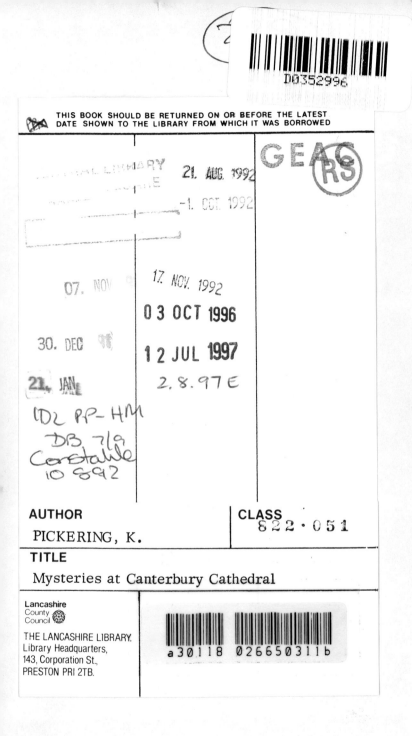

the high Summer of 1986 Marius Goring and other distin-
guished actors combined with the people of Canterbury to
present a new adaptation of THE MYSTERIES AT CANTER-
BURY CATHEDRAL.

Thousands of visitors from all parts of England and indeed
the world saw these fine performances and their full text is
now made available for a wider audience by Churchman
Publishing.

The script represents a unique collaboration between Kevin
Wood, the Artistic Director of a major professional Theatre
Company; Philip Dart, a talented young Director with wide
experience of touring theatre; and Kenneth Pickering, an
established authority on the Drama of the Christian Church,
with editorial supervision by Shirley Bennetts, Senior
Lecturer in Performing Arts at Nonington College, Kent.

Once again Canterbury Cathedral was the superb setting
for a remarkable collaboration of the Church and the Theatre
and the Citizens of Canterbury.

To Victor de Waal
a great encourager of the Arts

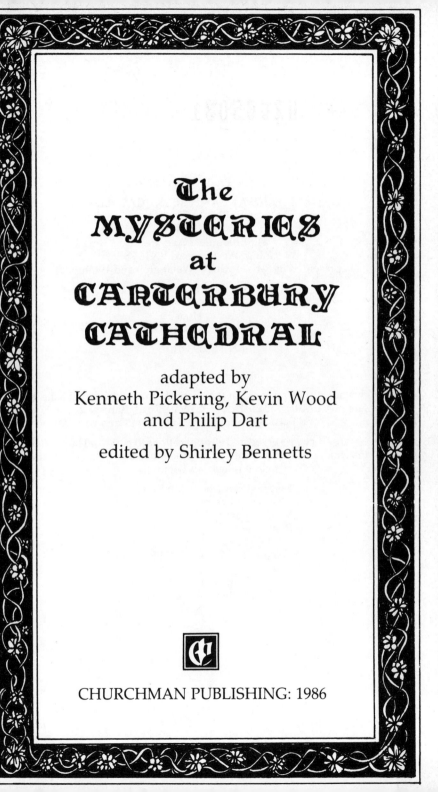

The MYSTERIES at CANTERBURY CATHEDRAL

adapted by
Kenneth Pickering, Kevin Wood
and Philip Dart

edited by Shirley Bennetts

CHURCHMAN PUBLISHING: 1986

02665031

THE MYSTERIES AT CANTERBURY CATHEDRAL
was first published in 1986 by
CHURCHMAN PUBLISHING LIMITED
117 Broomfield Avenue
Worthing, West Sussex, BN14 7SF
(Represented in Paris, Sydney, Wellington and Winnipeg)

and distributed to the book trade by
BAILEY BROS. & SWINFEN LIMITED
Warner House
Folkestone, Kent CT19 6PH

ISBN 1 85093 040 6

Made and printed in Great Britain by
Whitstable Litho Limited

Contents

These plays were first performed in Canterbury Cathedral on July 30th, 1986 with MARIUS GORING as GOD

Directors:	Kevin Wood
	Philip Dart
	Kenneth Pickering
Administrator:	Vanessa Mallatratt
Designer:	Helga Wood
Lighting Designer/Technician:	Dee Ashworth
Composer:	Keith Cole
Marketing:	John Curtin
Stage Manager	Vernon Marshal
Graphics:	John Gregson
Cast Co-ordinator:	Jim Vincent
Wardrobe Supervisor	Joyce Wood

THE COMPANY

Doug Alexander
Gina Allen
Maddy Allen
Julie Alston
Harold Anderton
Moira Arthurs
Joyce Ashton
Patricia Askew
Miriam August
Jeffrey Austen
Peter Austen
Lawrence Ayris
Melanie Baker
Valerie Bannister
Emmeline Barnett
David Barratt
Meg Baxter-Shaw
Steve Beasley
Meg Bennetts
Elsie Bentley
Pat Bestall
Rachel Bicker
Helen Bonnett
Clare Boulton
Juliet Britchford
Peter Brooks
Keiron Buffrey
Wendy Burnham
Cally Cameron
Thea Carr
William Carr
Zoe Carroll
Kevin Chalk
Robert Cherry
Julie Child
Sarah Churchward
Callum Coates
Jean Coates
Juliet Cole
Martyn Collins

Nick Collins
Ken Cooper
John Corbett
Geoff Cox
Veronica Cox
Frances Croskin
Jonathan Croskin
Karen Dadson
Katie Dane
Jenni Davis
Richard Davis
Carol Davis-Poynter
John Denton
Ann Dixon
Belinda Dixon
Jamie Eagle
Joseph Eagle
Marshall Eagle
Ben Earl
Joe Earl
Leah Earl
Patti Earl
Hugh Elsom
Mike England
Colin Eyre
Nigel Fairman
Maureen Fairweather
Johanna Falconer
Bill Fawcett
Philip Fearnall
Joy Fieldhouse
Daniel Fineman
Sally Fineman
Tessa Fineman
Julia Fleury
Katie Flook
Alison Foley
Madeleine Franklin
Reginald Franklin
Lucy Fredman

Sue Fredman
Daniel Freeman
Scarlett Freeman
Liz Friend
Joy Fryer
Maggie Gabbe
Sasha Gabbe
Samantha Gambrill
Jean Gil
Yvonne Gilbertson
Sally Glynn
Sue Goodwin
Geoff Goodwin
Scott Goodwin
Matthew Gordon
Sheila Gordon
Lynda Gray
Mary Grey
Daniel Harrington
Poppy Harris
Bob Higgins
Doreen Higgins
Edward Hill
Amy Hinchcliffe
Sally Hinchcliffe
Christine Hitchcock
Kirstie Hogarth
Lucy Holden
John Hole
Barry Hullett
Janet Hullett
Barbie Hunt
Liz Hurwitz
James Hyde
Jenny Ibbetson
Bridget Johnson
David Kemp
Bill Kenchington
Marion Kidder
Diana Knight

Helena Lacey
Duncan Langford
Madeleine Langford-Allen
Sally Lewis
Irene Lewis
Madeleine Lewis
Tedina Lineham
Charlotte Little
Georgina Little
Saskia Little
Margaret Lodge
Jeri Long
Jan Loveless
Alistair Macdonald
Geraldine Maple
Don Martin
Jo Martin
Kerry Martin
Maggie Martin
Rachel Martin
Lesley Martins
Deirdre Matheson
Zoe Matheson
Lynda Mills
Neil Mogridge
Clare Mole
Jo Moule
Kevin Mudge-Wood
Pam Mudge-Wood
Sally Naylor
Carol Newland
Dave Newland
Ursula Odendahl-Smith
Peggy O'Gara
Ann O'Hare

Alan Onions
Joyce Osborne
Alison Osmer
Carol Palmer
Joy Palmer
Peter Palmer
Susie Parfitt
David Paynter
Frances Pettett
Irene Pickering
Betty Pilcher
Bernard Plank
Lucinda Platt
Julie Platten
Shirley Platten
Susie Podmore
Wendy Podmore
Gina Poole
Mary Ray
Stuart Reid
John Roberts
Doreen Rosman
Elisabeth Rowe
Anita Salt
Dennis Saunders
Kerry Scamp
Chris Scott
Jennifer Sharman
Pat Simpson
Ben Slater
Elizabeth Smythe
Nicolette Sorba
Anita Spillet
Daniel Stanton
Jeama Stanton

Mandy Stanton
Mike Stanton
Lisa Terry
Robin Thompson
Helen Thorburn
Margaret Treacy
Liz Turner
Jayne Wackett
William Ward
Sara Warren
Chris Watson
Lynne Watson
Tim Watson
Fiona Watt
Mike Webb
Bridget Wells
Alison White
Andrew White
Joan White
Siobhan White
Jill Wiffin
Gezina Wilkinson
Sarah Williams
Carolyn Wing
Christine Wood
Elizabeth Wood
Emily Wood
George Wood
Joyce Wood
Margaret Wood
Ronald Wood
Ruth Wood
Gillian Worgan
John Wright

Preface

The cycles of plays performed on pageant wagons pulled through the streets of medieval towns and cities from one vantage point to another were known as 'mysteries'. Far from being strange tales with hidden meanings and unexpected endings, they took as their subject the familiar events of the Bible story, from the Creation to the Nativity, from the teachings and death of Christ to the Resurrection, the Ascension and the Last Day of Judgement. 'Mystery' was the Middle English word for a craft or a trade and it was the task of the trade guilds in these towns to mount the cycles. Each guild would undertake the production of one of the plays; we find 'The Crucifixion' being staged with grim appropriateness by the Pinners (Nailmakers) and Painters Guild in York, and 'Noah's Ark' being launched in the Chester cycle by the Waterleaders and Drawers of the River Dee. The cycles were performed for the people by the people, fleshing out in dramatic action the central truths of Christian teaching.

This popular tradition of drama, written in the vernacular and performed out in the streets, traced its descent, however, from within the church itself. For, as early as the tenth century, there is evidence of an exchange of responses in the Easter Mass where priests, intoning in Latin, took, as it were, the parts of Mary and the Angel/Gardener of Gethsemene. Soon there were shepherds represented in the Christmas service and it was not long before various locations in the nave and chancel were used and more elaborate tableaux were introduced.

Just how the drama moved out of the church and into the

streets is uncertain, and a matter of scholarly conjecture. One of the salient facts was the establishment early in the fourteenth century of the Feast of Corpus Christi, celebrated in the week following Trinity Sunday, a time when the hours of daylight were at their maximum and when the holy statues and treasures of the church could be paraded in processions round the town. From this solemn ritual it was a natural, if gradual, step to the vigorous celebration of the mystery plays – their other name being the Corpus Christi plays.

There are records of the existence of mystery cycles in over a hundred towns and cities in England alone, and there are cycles extant from York, Chester, Wakefield and from an East Midland 'N-town', as well as fragments from many other places. It is therefore very likely that Canterbury had its own cycle but at the present time this is still of a matter of supposition. Bafflingly, there are no references in the records to actual playtexts nor do the City Account Books reveal any payments towards the expenses of performance. Canterbury was not inimical to drama – far from it: the Prior of Christ Church made a payment out of his private account for a play in 1286; the Church Warden Account Inventory of St. Dunstan's records an 'Abraham and Isaac' and there are many references to Canterbury's own 'Pageant of St. Thomas'. In this, a hundred billmen and a hundred bowmen preceded a pageant wagon, which was refurbished in 1504. On it stood the figures of St. Thomas, with a mechanical moving head and a hidden bag of blood, and four boy knights with splendidly re-gilded armour. For our purposes, the real value in this record of 1504 lies in its mention of other pageant wagons preceding that of St. Thomas in the procession, carrying 'The Annunciation' and 'The Nativity'. Surely we can be allowed to see in these the relics of an indigenous Canterbury cycle?

With the Reformation came a reaction against not only the elaborate Church rituals but also the secular dramatic performances, and by the end of the sixteenth century, the City Fathers were paying troupes of players not to play but to move on. Church and theatre had parted company and were not to come together again until the twentieth century. Canterbury Cathedral was to play a vital role in the modern recognition of the value of drama in a religious framework, for it was here that, with the encouragement of the Dean, George Bell, the Canterbury Festival first began in 1928, enabling such commissioned works as T. S. Eliot's 'Murder in the Cathedral' and Dorothy Sayers' 'The Zeal of Thy House' to be staged within the precincts of the Cathedral.

Now in 1986, the mystery cycle has, as it were, come home. With the help of another Dean, Victor de Waal, the adaptors of this text were enabled to present a mystery play cycle for Canterbury in and about four different areas of the Cathedral. The glories of the mediaeval architecture provided a back drop to the glories of the mediaeval words, whilst the promenade nature of the performance allowed the audience to become part of the action, rubbing shoulders with the Disciples and processing with the Cross. Whilst the Nave provided polyscenic staging, the intimacy of the pageant wagon was achieved in the Crypt: Christ's cross was raised in the Cloister garden, stark against the summer evening sky, and across the Chapter House strode stern Old Testament figures.

This specially written script was arrived at by a free adaptation of the four major cycles, together with the use of mediaeval carols, verses of the Authorised Version of the Bible, Biblical paraphrase, newly composed songs and the occasional linking half-line. The individual episodes chosen allow the mediaeval writers' theological intentions to show more clearly than is often the case in cycle adaptations. We are able to see how Moses, in leading his people out of danger, prefigures Jesus, and to note how the story of Lazarus introduces the theme of the Resurrection. The authors were concerned to preserve the most vital features of the original, whilst ensuring that it did not become theatre archaeology, that there remained 'more of Carnival than of Evensong'. They have been at pains to maintain the vigour of the mediaeval metrical pattern and to this end have retained archaic words where these carry the alliterative stress or the rhyming pattern. To facilitate ready understanding, such words have been glossed in the body of the text, rather than in footnotes.

The 1986 script of the Canterbury Mysteries was the result of a collaboration between men of the theatre and of the study, the three bringing their preliminary work to fruition during the course of a long weekend closeted in a seaside hotel with a blizzard raging outside. The end product is truly a joint one, faithful to the spirit of collaboration evident in the original cycles.

This project would not have been possible without the help of the Dean and Chapter of Canterbury Cathedral; of the chief sponsor, the Kent Reliance Building Society; and of South East Arts: these bodies are today's equivalents of the mediaeval guildsmen and churchmen who instigated the original performances of the plays. At no time could the plays have been enacted without the presence in the production and in the audience of the people of Canterbury, to whom grateful thanks are offered.

The Creation

BANNS

EXPOSITOR:　Lordings royal and reverent,
　　　　Lovely ladies that here be lent,
　　　　Sovereign citizens, hither am I sent
　　　　A message for to say.
　　　　I pray you, all that be present,
　　　　That you will hear with good intent,
　　　　And let your ears to be lent
　　　　Willingly, I you pray.

　　　　Our worshipful Mayor of this city,
　　　　With all his goodly company,
　　　　Solemn pageants ordained hath he
　　　　Upon this eventide.
　　　　Whoso cometh these plays to see,
　　　　Heartily welcome shall he be,
　　　　And have right good cheer.

THE FALL OF LUCIFER

CHARACTERS

GOD
ANGEL(S)
LUCIFER
FALLEN ANGEL

THE FALL OF LUCIFER

GOD: I am the Alpha and Omega,
The first and the most famous.
It is my will it should be so,
It is, it was, it shall be thus.
I am great God gracious, which never had beginning,
I am maker unmade, all might is in me.
I am life and way unto wealth winning.
I am foremost and first, as I bid shall it be.
My blessing on blee shall be blending,   *bliss*
Where it shines, from all harm to be hiding,
My body in bliss aye abiding,
Unending, without any ending.

Since I am maker unmade and most is of might,
And aye shall be endless, and naught is but I,
Unto my dignity dear shall duly be dight   *made*
A place full of plenty to my pleasing at ply.
Now since I am thus solemn and set in my solation,
A bigly bliss here will I build, a heaven without ending,
And cast a comely compass to my comely creation,
Nine orders of angels be ever to one attending.

(*Angels sing; heavenly music.*)

Do your endeavour, and doubt ye not under my
    domination.
To sit in celestial safety, all solace to your sending,
For all the liking in this lordship be laud to my
    laudation.
Through the might of my most majesty your mirth shall
    ever be mending.
Here underneath me now an isle I neven,   *name*
Which isle shall be earth.

(*To* LUCIFER)

7

Of all the mights I have made most next after me,
I make thee as master and mirror of my might.
I bind thee here bainly, in bliss for to be,   *instantly*
I name thee for Lucifer, as bearer of light.

LUCIFER: Ah, merciful maker, full mickle is thy   *much*
    might,
That all this work at a word worthily had wrought.
Aye, loved be that lovely Lord of his light,
That us thus mighty have made, that now were right
    naught.

GOD: This work is now well wrought
    That is so clean and clear,
    As I made you of naught,
    My blessing I give you here.

(*Exit* GOD *while* LUCIFER *struts up and down and approaches*
GOD'*s vacant seat.*)

ANGELS: In bliss for to bide, in his blessing
    Aye – lasting, in love let us laud him,
    And dwell evermore thus about him,
    Of mirth nevermore to be missing.

LUCIFER: All the mirth that is made is marked in me!
    The beams of my bright head are burning so bright!
    And I so seemly in sight myself now I see
    For like a lord am I left to lend in this light.   *dwell*

    More fairer by far than my feres,   *companions*
    In me is no point that may pair;   *deteriorate*
    I feel me featous and fair,   *comely*
    My power is passing my peers.

(*As he is about to sit on throne,* GOD *appears.*)

GOD: Now, since I have formed you so fair,
    And exalted you so excellent,
    And here I see you next my chair,
    My love to you is so fervent,
    Look ye fall not in despair,
    Touch not my throne by no assent.
    All your beauty I shall impair
    If pride prove now your true intent.

LUCIFER: Nay, Lord, that would I not indeed,
           For none may trespass unto thee;
           Thy great godhead thus will we dread
           And never exalt ourselves so free.

GOD: Now I will wend and take my trace   *go*
       And see this bliss in every tower.
       Each one of you keep well his place,
       And Lucifer, I make thee governor.
       Behold the beams of my bright face
       Which ever was and shall endure.

       (GOD *goes*.)

LUCIFER: Ah, Ah! That I am wondrous bright
           Among you all – shining so clear –
           Of all heaven I bear the light,
           Though God himself were even here!

           All in his throne if that I were
           Then should I be as wise as he,
           What say you, angels, all that be here?
           Some homage soon now let me see!

           (ANGELS *confer*.)

ANGEL: We will not assent unto your pride,
         Nor in our hearts take such a thought,
         But that our Lord shall be our guide
         And keep to us what he hath wrought.

           LUCIFER: Distress! I command you all to cease,
           And see the beauty that I bear;
           All heaven shines through my brightness,
           For God himself shines not so clear.
           Here will I sit now in this stid   *fashion*
           To exalt myself in this same seat.

           (LUCIFER *sits on* GOD's *throne*.)

           Behold my body, both hand and head,
           All angels turn to me, I redd,   *order*
           And to your sovereign kneel on your knee,
           I am your comfort both lord and head,
           The mirth and the might of the majesty.

9

(*One only kneels.* LUCIFER *stands, furious.*)

I redd you all, do my reverence.   *order*
I am replete with heavenly grace.
Though God come here, I will not hence
But sit right here before his face.

(LUCIFER *sits back on the throne.* GOD *re-enters.*)

GOD: Say, what array do you make here?
Where is your prince and principal?

(*They all tremble.*)

I made thee an angel, Lucifer,
And here thou would be lord over all?
Therefore I charge this order clear;
Fast from this place, look that ye fall.
I made thee my friend, thou art my foe,
Why hast thou trespassed thus to me?
I charge you now, fall till I bid 'No'!
To the pit of hell, evermore to be!

(LUCIFER *and the* FALLEN ANGEL *are cast down into Hell.*)

LUCIFER: Oh deuce! All goes down:
My might and my main are all marrand;   *destroyed*
Help fellows, in faith I am falland!

FALLEN ANGEL: Alas! That ever we were wrought!
That we should come into this place!
We were in joy, now we be naught.
Alas, we have forfeited our grace!

LUCIFER: Out, out! Harrow! Helpless – so hot it is here!
This is a dungeon of dole that I am to dight.   *cast into*

FALLEN ANGEL: And even hither thou hast us brought
Into this dungeon to take our trace.
All this sorrow thou hast it sought;
The devil may speed thy stinking face!

LUCIFER: My brightness is blackest and blue now;
My bale is aye beating and burning.
Woe, woe is me! Now it is worse than it was!

FALLEN ANGEL: Thou hast brought us this wicked way.

10

LUCIFER: Ye lie! Out, alas!
    I wist not this woe should be wrought,
    Out on you, lurdan, ye smore me in smoke!   *smother*

(They go out, choking in smoke.)

GOD: Ah, wicked pride, aye worth thee woe!
    They would not me worship that wrought them.
    Henceforth shall my wrath ever go with them,
    And all that me worship shall abide here in bliss.
    Now more of my work, for work now I will.

(GOD moves to another place.)

THE CREATION
OF ADAM AND EVE

CHARACTERS

GOD
ADAM
EVE

THE CREATION OF ADAM AND EVE

GOD: See, Heaven and Hell are made in my might.
In Heaven are angels both fair and bright,
But Earth in its void is dark as the night.
I bid, in my blessing, ye angels give light
For when the fiend fell it faded from sight.

For name, let darkness be known as 'the night',
And 'day' is the name I give to the light.

(*The Earth is lit.*)

Now for my purpose I twin them in two.
In Heaven, the planets and stars will shine through
And greater lights more than ever I knew
Named 'sun' and named 'moon' each other pursue.
The sun for the day, the moon for the night
Thus they are divided, and give there some light.

On earth shall be wetness – and dry I install.
The gathering of wet, 'sea' shall I call,
Therein shall swim fishes and whales, great and small,
And from earth shall spring grass and trees diverse tall,
And beasts, fowls and insects about them will crawl.
Thus the world is created. In five days, I recall.

To keep this world, both more and less,
A skilful beast now will I make
After my shape and my likeness,
To worship me. And, for his sake,
Of the simplest part of earth that is here
I shall make Man.
Therefore rise up, O earth, in blood and bone,
In shape of man! I here command!

(ADAM *rises from the earth.*)

Take now this ghost of life
And receive your soul from me.

(GOD *breathes on* ADAM.)

15

ADAM: Lord, full mickle is thy might   *great*
   And that is seen on every side;
   For now is here a joyful sight,
   To see this world so long and wide.

GOD: A female shalt thou have as mate
   'She' shall I make of thy left rib.
   Alone so shalt thou not long wait
   Without a faithful friend and sib.   *relation*

(EVE *rises from the earth.*)

This woman take thou as thy wife
And 'Adam' and 'Eve', your names for life.

(GOD *breathes on* EVE. *She sees* GOD *and* ADAM. ADAM *and* EVE *hold hands.*)

ADAM: Many dyvers thing there is
   Of beasts and fowls, both wild and tame;
   Yet is none made to thy likeness
   But we alone. Praised be thy name!

EVE: To such a Lord in all degree
   Be evermore lasting loving,
   That to us such a dignity
   Has given before all other things.

ADAM: Ah, blessed Lord! Now from the day
   Since we are wrought, vouchsafe to tell
   What we must do, and also say,
   Most gracious Lord, where we must dwell.

GOD: In Paradise shall ye both dwell,
   A place of pleasure and delight.
   My name to worship evermore,
   As all things else will *thee* adore.

Of all the trees that be herein
Thou mayest eat fruit and know no sin.
But from this single tree alone
If thou shouldst eat, fall from thy throne!

ADAM: Ah, Lord, since we shall do nothing
   But love thee for thy great goodness,
   We shall obey to thy bidding,

EVE: And keep thy word both more and less.

GOD: With heaven and earth first I began
And my creation all was blessed.
The sixth day, I created Man,
And on the seventh will I rest.

To bliss I shall ye bring;
Come forth ye two, with me.
Ye shall live in loving;
My blessings with you be.

(*Exeunt* GOD, ADAM *and* EVE.)

THE FALL OF MAN

CHARACTERS

LUCIFER
EVE
ADAM
GOD
ANGEL

THE FALL OF MAN

LUCIFER: Alas for me! This Hell is hot!
    Ah, Lucifer, is this thy lot?
    I, that sat so close to God,
    Am pinched and cramped, with pitchforks prod.
    I, that ruled most bright and fair,
    An angel high without compare,
    Am fell from grace; vaunting ambition
    Hath brought me to this sad condition.
    And in my stead, a master new
    God has made, His work to do,
    By His own hand, the man is put
    To rule o'er earth, while I in soot
    Have lost the bliss that should be mine,
    The noble trust, and love divine.
    But harken all to what I say!
    If I have sinned, then I repay.
    I, Lucifer, exiled from light,
    Shall all the bliss of mankind blight.
    To Adam's mate now will I hie,
    With serpent's guise to charm her eye.
    In a worm's likeness will I wend.
    Eve! Eve!

EVE: Who is there?

LUCIFER: 'Tis I, a friend.
    And for thy good is my coming.
    Of all the fruit that here doth grow
    Why eat ye naught, I beg to know?

EVE: We may of them each one
    Take all that us good thought,
    Save one tree out is ta'en
    Would do harm to nigh it aught.

LUCIFER: And why that tree – that would I wit –   *know*
    Any more than all other by?

EVE: For our Lord God forbids us it

The fruit thereof, Adam nor I,
To nigh it near;   *approach*
And if we did, we both should die,
He said, and cease our solace here.

LUCIFER: Yea, Eve, to me take tent,   *pay attention*
Take heed, and thou shalt hear
What he by those words meant.
Come close, there's naught to fear.
To eat thereof he you forfend.   *forbad*
I know it well, this was his skill,
Because he would none other kenned   *knew*
Those great virtues that are there still.
For wilt thou see?
Who eats the fruit of good and ill
Shall have knowing as well as he.   *knowledge*

EVE: What kind of thing art thou
That tells this tale to me?

LUCIFER: A worm that knows well how
That ye may worshipped be.

(*He genuflects.*)

EVE: What worship should we win thereby?
To eat thereof us needeth it naught.
We had lordship to make mastery,
O'er all things that in earth is wrought.

LUCIFER: Woman, do way!

EVE: To do is us full loathe,
That should our God mispay.

LUCIFER: Nay, certes, it is no wothe,   *certainly; harm*
Eat it safely ye may.
For peril right none therein lies,
But worship and a great winning.
For right as God, ye shall be wise,
And peer to him in everything.
Aye, Gods shall ye be.

EVE: Is this true that thou says?

LUCIFER: Yea, why trustest thou not me?
    I would by no kin ways   *by no means*
    Tell I naught but truth to thee.

EVE: Then will I to thy teaching trust
    And fang this fruit into our food.   *take*

(*She takes the apple from the tree.*)

LUCIFER: Bite on boldly, be not abashed.

(EVE *bites apple.*)

Now to Adam, to share your bliss.

(LUCIFER *laughs and retires.*)

EVE: Adam, have here of fruit full good.

ADAM: Alas woman, why took'st thou this?
    Our Lord commanded us both
    To tent this tree of his.   *heed*
    Thy work will make him wroth: *angry*
    Alas, thou'st done amiss!

EVE: Nay, Adam grieve thee not at this,
    And I shall say the reason why.
    A worm has shown eternal bliss.
    We shall be as Gods, thou and I,
    If that we eat,
    Here of this tree. Adam, thereby
    Let not that worship for to get,
    For we shall be as wise
    As God that is so great,
    And as mickle of prize;
    Therefore eat thou of this meat.

ADAM: To eat it would I not refuse
    Could I be sure of thy saying.

EVE: Bite on boldly, for it is true:
    We shall be gods and know all things.

(ADAM *bites the apple.*)

ADAM: Alas, what have I done? For shame!

23

Ill counsel! Woe be to thee!
Ah, Eve, thou art to blame;
To this enticed thou me.
My body does me shame,
For I am naked, as methink.

EVE: Alas, Adam, right so am I.

ADAM: And for sorrow sore, why might we not sink?
For we have grieved God Almighty
That made me Man,
Broken his bidding bitterly.   *grievously*
Alas, that ever we began
This work Eve, and wrought
And made this bad bargain!

EVE: Nay Adam, blame me naught.

ADAM: Go way, Eve love, who then?

EVE: The worm, alas, well worthy were.
With tales untrue, he me betrayed.

ADAM: Alas, that I list to thy lore,
Or tent the trifles that thou me said.   *believed; lies*
Our shapes for shame me grieve;
With what shall they be hid?

EVE: Take us these fig leaves
Since it is thus betid.   *happened*

ADAM: Right as thou say'st, so shall it be,
For we are naked and all bare.
Full wonder fain I would hide me
From my Lord's sight – if I knew where.

(GOD *appears*.)

GOD: Adam!

ADAM: Lord?

GOD: Where art thou? Yare!   *quickly*

ADAM: I hear thee, Lord, but see thee naught.
I am naked as the day is long.

GOD: This work, what hast thou wrought?

ADAM: Lord, Eve it was made me do wrong,
And to this breach me brought.   *breach of duty*

GOD: Eve, why didst thou give thy mate
Fruit I bid thee should hang still,
And commanded none to take?

EVE: This work, Lord, enticed me theretill.
Oh welaway!   *alas*
That ever I did that deed so dill!   *foolish*

GOD: Ah wicked worm, woe worth thee ay!
For thou on this manner
Hast made them such affray.
My malice have thou here
With all the might I may.
Hence on thy womb now shalt thou glide,
Cursed shalt thou be, for sake of Eve.

(LUCIFER *falls onto his stomach and slithers away hissing.*)

And, woman I warn thee wytterlie,   *surely*
Thy mischief I shall multiply.
Henceforth, with pain, and great annoy
Thy children shalt thou bear.
And for that thou hast done today
The Man shall master thee alway.
Under his power now shalt thou be.
And Adam, henceforth I say to thee,
In Middle-Earth now sweat and swink,   *toil*
And travail for thy food.

ADAM: Oh master, what has befall? Why is it that we sink?
We that had all earthly bliss
Have now good cause to think.

GOD: Ho, Cherubim! Mine angel bright
To Middle-Earth go drive these two.

ANGEL: All ready Lord, and it is right
Since thy will is that, it must be so.
Adam and Eve with me now go,

25

Thy sorrow I am telling.
Come forth, come fast, to Middle-Earth
For here make ye no dwelling.

ADAM: Alas, for life! Alas, for woe!
Come wife, 'tis done, 'tis meet we go.

CAIN AND ABEL

CHARACTERS

PIKHARNESSE
CAIN
ABEL
GOD

CAIN AND ABEL

(*Horse dance is in progress as the audience enters. A boy comes forward.*)

PIKHARNESS: Now here I am, a merry boy,
All hail, all hail! Be full of joy,
Shut your noise and listen to me,
And hear what you are about to see.
Make way, make way for Adam's sons,
For Cain and Abel are about to come!
One with plough, the other with sheep.
Now see how well God's law they keep.

(CAIN *enters ploughing; he is having considerable trouble in making the horses work.*)

CAIN: Hey up Greenham! Come on Gryne,
Quickly now, waste not my time!
Plough this field today we must,
Move you now, with wrath I bust!
Oh, you nags, will you not work?
Now pull this way and do not shirk.
What are you doing standing still?
O, hang for you I surely will!

Pikharness, Pikharness, my servant lad!

PIK: Greetings to thee master, be ever glad!

CAIN: How is't you are never near at hand?
Come on now, make them plough the land!

PIK: Come on now Mull! Oh, come on Stott,
You know that ploughing is your lot.

(*Horses start to move.*)

Now you see they work for me,
'Tis just they will not move for thee.

CAIN: Pikharness, thou art a cheeky lad!
Your cockiness doth make me mad!

29

Oh, how I wish that thee were dead,
I must tan your hide instead!
I am your master; will you fight?

PIK: Yes, unless thou takest fright,
When I shall show you all my might!

(*Comic fight,* CAIN *missing the faster* PIK.)

PIK: (*Seeing* ABEL *coming.*)

Ah, but look yonder, I see your kin,
Your brother Abel comes here for worshipping.
This bantering must now surely stop.

CAIN: Oh, to hell with you and there to rot!

ABEL: God, as He both may and can,
Speed you, brother, and your man.

CAIN: Come kiss my arse! I will not ban.   *curse*
Away from here is your welcome.
Go off with you, dear brother, and kiss the devil's bum.
Why sneak up like a thief?
When I want you, I will shout.

ABEL: Brother, there is none about
Would cause you any grief.
But my brother, hear me more,
For it is the custom of our law
That all whose works and ways are nice
Shall worship God with sacrifice.
And, therefore, brother, let us pray
That God may clean our hearts this day.
Then make our offering should we,
Of corn or cattle it can be.
So God may his great mercy send
To grant us bliss without an end.

CAIN: On, and on, and on, you preach!
How long these lessons will you teach?
For God's sake hold your tongue, I say,
Or else go work the Devil's way!
Should I leave my plough and everything

30

And go with thee to make an offering?
You will not find me that mad,
Go to the Devil and say I'm bad!
What does God give to make you praise Him so?
He gives me naught but sorrow and woe.

ABEL: Cain, this talk is vanity,
God gives your livelihood to you.

CAIN: Yet not a farthing do I see.
What He gives have I no clue!

ABEL: Our custom, brother, doth require
A tenth of all our stock entire
To be, in God's name, burned with fire.

CAIN: Huh, what is to you to tithe, dear brother,
For me each year is worse than the other.
So little can I glean
No wonder I be lean!
Yet if a fat gift I could bring,
He would not lend me anything.

ABEL: Yet everything that you do own
Is of God's good grace, and a loan.

CAIN: What reason have I to think that so
Since I remember He was my foe?
If indeed He was my friend,
There was plenty He could lend.
When all men's corn was fair in field
Not a penny's worth was my yield!
When I would sow and wanted seed,
And of corn had the greatest need,
Then He gave me not a jot.
So, now I keep what I have got!

ABEL: Cain, dear brother, say not so,
But let us forth together go.

(CAIN *does not move.*)

Dear Cain, it would grieve my heart
If you and I should go apart.

31

The ties of blood do not deny;
Are we not brothers, you and I?

CAIN: I would not part to please God or not
With anything that I have got.
But I suppose I cannot win,
So to your pleas I will give in.
Lead on – though I am loathe to go.

ABEL: Dear brother Cain, why are you so?
Come! Let us journey onward together.
Blessed is God; we have fine weather.

(*They move to the place of sacrifice,* ABEL *with sheep and* CAIN *with corn.*)

CAIN: Lay down your bundle upon this hill.

ABEL: Forsooth, brother, so I will.
And, God of heaven, take it good.

CAIN: Now offer first your livelihood.

ABEL: God, that created both earth and sky,
I pray to thee to hear my cry.
Now, take with thanks if 'tis thy will,
This tithe I offer here on this hill.
For I give it to thee with good intent,
To thee, my Lord, that all hath sent.
I burn it now with steadfast thought
In worship of Him that all hath wrought.

(*White smoke appears.*)

CAIN: Rise! Let me, since you have done,
Quickly finish what is begun.
Yet, as I stand here with these shanks,
I have no cause to give much thanks.
I know however much I burn
Will bring no profit in return.
Although to tithe I have no heart,
I suppose I had better make a start.

(CAIN *begins to count the sheaves but deliberately miscounts and holds back the best ones for himself.*)

One sheaf, one; and this makes two!
Neither can I spare for you.
Ah, here! Another making three,
Yet also, this shall stay with me.
For I will choose these three to keep,
He shall not have the best I reap.

(*Selecting a very poor sheaf*)

Ah, take this one, Lord, as thy due,
For this is all I give to you!

ABEL: Cain, be advised and tithe aright.
Fear you not God in all his might?

CAIN: My tithing need not lose you sleep,
Be off and tend thy scabby sheep.
For if you would meddle more with me
Then it will be the worse for thee.
Four, five, six; and seven –
Oh, go not these to God in heaven!
Seven . . . seven. Now this is eight.

ABEL: Cain, brother, beware God's hate.

CAIN: None of these here on my right
Shall ever come into God's sight.
Oh, come fire, burn bright, I say,
Receive the tithe I give today.
Oh, this smoke does me much shame.
Now, burn, I say, in the Devil's name!

(*Black smoke appears.*)

Cursed be this stink I smell,
'Tis not from heaven but sure from hell!
Had I but taken one breath more,
I had been choked, and that right sore.

ABEL: Cain, for nothing do you choke,
A true tithe burns without black smoke.

CAIN: Come, kiss the devil in the arse!
Because of thee, it burns the worse.
Would that within thy cursed throat,

33

Were fire and smoke to stop thy note.

(GOD *appears*.)

GOD: Cain, why are you thus so stirred
Against your brother Abel's word?
For, since no man can me deceive,
As he shall give, he shall receive.

(GOD *withdraws*.)

CAIN: Phew! Who is that hob over the wall?
Who was that, that piped so small?
Old God must be out of His wit
But surely now we had better flit.
For certain, Old God is not my friend.
Come on, Abel, away let us wend.   *90*

ABEL: Ah, brother Cain, for you I grieve.

CAIN: No, come on, Abel, let us leave,
To find some place, where it may be
That God no more can look on me.

ABEL: Brother, I will not journey far,
Only to where the cattle are.
For all need food and some are sick.

CAIN: No, stop! I have a bone to pick!
A villain's plan you now are shaping,
Your mind is set not on escaping!
No, I owe you many a crack,
The time has come to pay you back.

ABEL: Why do you rage at me and sneer?

CAIN: Why? Why? Burned your tithe so clear?
Yet my offering never more than smoked,
And, dear brother, I nearly choked!

ABEL: So doth the will of God appear,
'Twas He that made my tithe burn clear.
If yours but only smoked – am I to blame?

CAIN: Why yes! And I will stop your game.

34

(CAIN *picks up a large bone and threatens* ABEL.)

May this cheek bone burst your brain,
That life and you shall part in twain!

(CAIN *attacks* ABEL *with a bone;* ABEL *falls to the ground.*)

Lie down there and take your rest,
I'll now be rid of thee – thou pest!

ABEL: Vengeance! Vengeance, Lord I cry,
For I am slain and guiltless die!

(ABEL *dies.*)

CAIN: (*To audience*)

And if you lot say I did wrong,
Beware of me; my arm is strong!

(GOD *appears.*)

GOD: Cain! Cain!

CAIN: Who is that who calleth me?
I am here, canst thou not see?

GOD: Cain, where does your brother Abel dwell?

CAIN: Why ask me? Maybe in hell!
Or somewhere he may lie sleeping,
Is my brother in my keeping?

GOD: No longer, Cain, can you lie or boast;
I hear the voice of your brother's ghost.
Ye have him slain, I know your lies.
From earth to heaven 'vengeance' cries!
Your sin of all sins is the worst,
And henceforth ye shall be accursed.

(ANGEL *marks* CAIN.)

CAIN: Since I have done so great a sin
That I may never thy mercy win;
Since you have banished me from grace,
Now will I hide me from thy face:
So any man that I may meet,

35

In country way or city street,
Wherever wretched Cain is found,
There let him strike me to the ground,
And bury me in ditch or bog,
Despised, cast out, like some dead dog.

GOD: No, Cain, it shall be as I will;
No man his brother man should kill.
He that slayeth, young or old,
He shall be punished sevenfold.

NOAH'S FLOOD

CHARACTERS

GOD
NOAH
SHEM
HAM
JAPHETH
SHEM'S WIFE
HAM'S WIFE
JAPHETH'S WIFE
NOAH'S WIFE

NOAH'S FLOOD

GOD: I, God, that all the world have wrought,
       And Heaven and Earth, and all from nought,
       Now see my people, in deed and thought,
       Are foully set in sin.
       Man that I made I will destroy,
       Beast, worm, and fowls that fly;
       For on Earth they do me noy,   *harm*
       The folk that are therein.

       Therefore, Noah, my servant free,
       A righteous man thou art I see,
       A ship soon thou shalt make thee
       Of trees dry and light.
       Little chambers therein thou make;
       And binding pitch also thou take;
       Within and without do not slake   *slacken*
       To make it with all thy might.

       Three hundred cubits it shall be long,
       And fifty of breadth to make it strong,
       Of height thirty, and be not wrong.
       Thus measure it about.
       One window, work through thy wit,
       A cubit of length and breadth make it;
       Upon the side a door shall sit,
       For to come in and out.

       Eating places thou make also,
       Three roofed chambers in a row;
       For with water I mean to flow
       O'er Man that I did make.
       Destroyed all the world shall be,
       Save thou; thy wife, thy sons three,
       And all their wives also with thee,
       Shall saved be, for thy sake.

NOAH: Ah, Lord, I thank thee loud and still,
        That spares me and my kin from spill.

Thy bidding, Lord, I shall fulfill,
And set about it now.

(*Exit* GOD.)
Hie thou, ye men and women all!
Saved we be from aught befall.
So work this ship, chamber and hall,
As thou didst hear me vow.

SHEM: Father, we are all ready boun.   *prepared*
An axe I have, by my crown,
As sharp as any in this town;
This pledge I to this task.

HAM: I have a brace and bit with me,
That wouldst bit int' the hardest tree,
A better grounden thou't not see.   *sharpened*
I do what thou does ask.

JAPHETH: And I can well make a pin,
And with this hammer knock it in.
None there will be shall make more din
Than I, to build this ark.

SHEM'S WIFE: And we shall bring timber too,
For we mun nothing else to do,   *may*
Women are weak to undergo
The building of this barque.

HAM'S WIFE: Here is a sturdy chopping block,
On this may ye all hew and knock
Till none be idle in this flock.
God's blessing we shall win.

JAPHETH'S WIFE: And I will gather splinters here
To make a fire for you in fere   *company*
And on't I'll cook for all a dinner
Against you may come in.

(ALL *set to work with tools.*)

NOAH: Now, in the name of God, we begin
To make this ship, for to live in
That we be ready for to swim

40

At the coming of the flood.
These boards we join here together
To keep us safe from the weather,
That we may row both hither and thither,
And safe be from this flood.

Of this tree, we'll make the mast,
Tied with cables that will last,
With a sail yard for each blast,
And each thing in their kind.
With topcastle, and bowsprit,
With cords and ropes, still coiled as yet,
We set forth, with the next wet.
This ship is at an end.

Wife in this ship we'll be safe kept,
My children and thou, aboard now step.

NOAH'S WIFE: Husband, thou may'st have well o'erslept
If thou think'st thou can'st scare.
I will not in that ark be hid.

NOAH: Good wife, do now as I thee bid!

NOAH'S WIFE: By Christ, not till I see more need,
Though thou may stand all day and stare!

GOD: Noah, take thou thy meny,   *household*
And in the ship hie that thou be;
For none so righteous man to me
Is now on earth living.
Of beasts take thou two and two,
Male and female, with none mo,
List well this plan that thou shalt do,
Against I send the weather.

Seven days be yet coming;
You shall have space them in to bring.
After that, it is my liking
Mankind for to noy.   *harm*
Forty days and forty nights
Rain shall fall for their unrights,
And that I made through all my might
Now think I to destroy.

NOAH: Lord, at your bidding I am bain,   *ready*
        Since none other grace will gain,
        I fulfill it without pain,
        For gracious I thee find.

        (*Exit* GOD.)

        Have done, ye men and women all!
        Hie ye, lest this water fall!
        Bring to the ship beasts great and small,
        Two now of every kind.

SHEM: Sir, here are lions, leopards in,
        Horses, mares, oxen and swine,
        Goats, calves, sheep, and kine
        Here sitten thou may see.

HAM: Camels, asses men may find,

JAPHETH: Buck, doe, hart and hind;

JAPHETH'S WIFE: And beasts of all manner kind,
        Here be, as thinkest me.

SHEM'S WIFE: Take here cats and dogs too,
        Otter, fox, fulmart also;   *polecat*
        Hares, hopping gaily go,

JAPHETH'S WIFE: Here's cole for them to eat.   *cabbage*

HAM'S WIFE: And here are bears, wolves set,
        Apes, owls, marmoset,

JAPHETH: Weasels, squirrels and ferrets,
        Here they'll eat their meat.

HAM: Yet more beasts are in this house,
        Here cats making it full crouse,   *a lively time*

JAPHETH'S WIFE: Here a ratton, here a mouse,   *rat*
        They stand nigh together.

SHEM: And here are fowls, less and more:
        Herons, cranes and bittor,   *bittern*

SHEM'S WIFE: Swans, peacocks; and set before
        Food against this weather.

JAPHETH: Here are cocks, kites, crows,

HAM'S WIFE: Rooks and ravens, many rows,

HAM: Ducks, curlews, whoever knows.
    One of every kind.

JAPHETH'S WIFE: And here are doves, digs, drakes,   *ducks*

SHEM: Redshanks running from the lakes,

NOAH: Each fowl and beast that God did'st make,
    In this ship men may find.

    Wife, come in! Why stands thou there?
    This is no time for moods, I swear.
    Come in, on God's behest, my dear,
    For fear lest that you drown!

NOAH'S WIFE: Yea sir, set up thy sail,
    Go forth with evil hail!
    For, without any fail,
    I will not leave this town.

    Without my gossips, every one,
    One foot further, I will not gone.
    They loved me full well, by Christ!
    Unless thou let them on thy list,
    Thou may row forth, Noah, where 'er thou wist,
    And get thee a new wife.

NOAH: Shem, son, Lo! Thy mother is wrow,   *angry*
    Forsooth, such another I do not know.

SHEM: Father, I shall fetch her in, I trow,   *think*
    Without any fail.
    Mother, my father me after thee did send,
    And bids thee into yon ship wend,   *go*
    Look up and see this angry wind.
    'Tis time that we set sail.

NOAH'S WIFE: Son, go again to him, and say
    I will not come therein today.

NOAH: Come in, wife, in twenty devils' way,
    Or else stand there without!

HAM: Shall we all fetch her in?

NOAH: Good sons, with Christ's blessing and mine,
     I wish you would and in quick time,
     For of this flood, there is no doubt.

GOSSIP: Lo, water comes fleeting in full fast,   *flowing*
     On every side it spreads full far,
     For fear of drowning I am aghast,
     Good gossip, let us draw near!

NOAH'S WIFE: And let us drink ere down we go;
     For oft times past we have done so,
     Here is my bottle of Malmsey, lo!
     We'll drown ourselves in cheer.

JAPHETH: Mother, we pray you, all together,
     For we are here, your three childer,
     Come inside, for fear of the weather,
     For God's love that you bought.

NOAH'S WIFE: That will I not, for all you call
     Until I have my gossips all.

SHEM: In good faith, mother, that you shall
     Whether you will or nought.

     (SHEM *lifts his* MOTHER *up and carries her aboard*.)

NOAH: Ah, welcome, wife, into this ship!

NOAH'S WIFE: Here, take thou this for thy tip!

     (NOAH'S WIFE *hits* NOAH.)

NOAH: Ho, what? Methinks my boat did dip.
     God do as Thou will.
     This window will I shut anon,
     And into my chamber will I be gone
     Till this water has become
     More slaked by thy skill.   *lessened*

     (NOAH *closes the window. Time passes.* NOAH *opens the window*.)

     Now, forty days are fully gone,

44

A raven will I send anon,
To see if aught where tree or stone
Be dry in any place.
And if this fowl come not again,
It is a sign, sooth to sayn,
That dry it is on hill or plain
And God hath shown some grace.

(*He releases a raven.*)

Good Lord, where'er this raven be
Somewhere is dry land I see;
So now a dove I will set free
A messenger to send.
Thou wilt return again to me.
For, of all fowls that may flee
O'er land and o'er this mighty sea,
Thou art most meek and hend.   *gentle*

(NOAH *releases a dove and it returns with an olive branch.*)

Ah, Lord, blessed be Thou aye
That me has comforted this today!
For by this sight I may well say
This flood begins to cease.
My sweet dove to me brought has
A branch of olive from some place,
And this betokeneth God's good grace,
And is a sign of peace.

GOD: Noah, take thy wife anon,
And thy chidren every one,
Out of thy ship thou shalt be gone,
And they alone with thee.
Beasts and all the fowls that fly
Out anon, they shall hie,
On earth to grow and multiply,
I will that it so be.

Weary earth will I no more
For man's sin that grieves me sore,
For, from his youth and e'en before,
Man sinned against my will.

Here I beheet thee a hest,   *make you a promise*
That man, woman, fowl nor beast,
With water, whilst the world shall last,
I vow no more to spill.

A rainbow set 'twixt thou and me
In the firmament shall be,
To be a token that all may see,
My vengeance now shall cease.
And man nor woman never more
Be wasted by water, as was before,
For sin that grieveth me full sore,
Therefore this vengeance was.

My blessings now I give thee here,
To thee, Noah, my servant dear,
For vengeance shall no more appear,
And now farewell, my darling dear.

ABRAHAM AND ISAAC

CHARACTERS

EXPOSITOR
ABRAHAM
GOD
SARAH
ISAAC

ABRAHAM AND ISAAC

EXPOSITOR: All peace, Lordings, that be present
And hasten now with good intent,
Now Noah away from us is went,   *gone*
And all his company:
And Abraham, through God's good grace,
Is coming to this very place,
And you must give him room and space
To tell you his story.

(ABRAHAM *enters to pray*.)

ABRAHAM: Father of Heaven Magnificent,
With all my heart to thee I call.
Thou hast given me land and rent,
And my livelihood hast sent.
I thank thee highly, evermore, for all.

Now I am old, my joy is this;
That thou did grant me my sweet son.
No other joy would I so miss
Except thyself, dear Father of Bliss,
As little Isaac, my own dear one.

And, therefore, Father of Heaven, I pray
For his health and for his grace,
Now, Lord, keep him both night and day,
That no disease or danger may
Come to my child in any place.

(*In Heaven* GOD *speaks to an* ANGEL.)

GOD: Mine Angel, fast be on your way
Down to earth to do my will.
Try the heart of Abraham I say
And prove if he be steadfast still.

Say I command him now to take
Isaac, the son he loves so deep,
And with his love an offering make,
If that my friendship he would keep.

49

Show him the way on to the hill,
Where this sacrifice shall be.
There my command he shall fulfill,
And choose between his child and me.

(ANGEL *leaves Heaven.*
Back on earth, ABRAHAM *is still praying.*)

ABRAHAM: Now, Father of Heaven, who formed all thing,
My prayers I make to thee once more,
For today a tender offering
I must give to thee for sure.
What manner of beast is thy desiring?
For obediently I shall obtain,
To sacrifice to thee, Almighty King,
In some high place above the plain.

(ANGEL *arrives from Heaven.*)

ANGEL: Abraham, Abraham, why do you rest?
Our Lord commands for you to take
Isaac, the young son you love the best,
And with his blood an offering make.
Go, climb up high the yonder hill,
And give your child unto the Lord.
There your dear one's blood must spill.
Unto God's will you must accord.

ABRAHAM: Welcome, Angel, whom God has sent.
I know your bidding must be done.
It is ever my wish to be obedient,
Yet, hear a plea for my dearest one.

If it could please Lord God on high
To take instead all I possess,
And tell me Isaac need not die,
My heart would leap with happiness.

For I love Isaac as much as life,
But yet I love my God the more.
Though my heart should burst with strife
I will do God's will and keep his law.

Thus, although my grief can never heal,

I shall cut off my Isaac's head,
O, Father of Heaven to whom I kneel
All honour be, O Lord most dread.

ANGEL: Abraham, Abraham, this is well said,
And all these commandments look that thou keep.
And by God's will henceforth be led.
Go forth, there is no cause to weep.

(*The* ANGEL *departs.*)

ABRAHAM: Although my heart be heavy and sad
To see the blood of my dear son,
I know I must go fetch the lad
And see that sacrifice be done.

Oh, but what my wife to tell?
Her life on Isaac doth depend.
To slay the son she loves so well –
Her bitter grief would never end.

(*Enter* SARAH *with* ISAAC.)

SARAH: Welcome my Lord, now home at last!
Oh, you have been too long away!
Come, tell me, quickly, what has passed.
Sweet, tell us what you have to say.

ABRAHAM: Dear, nothing happened untoward!
Save that an Angel to me came,
Who brought instruction from the Lord,
For sacrifice above this plain.

Isaac, dress and come with me,
And we will climb on yonder heights,
For it is meet that thou should see
Observance of these holy rites.

ISAAC: Oh yes, my Father, let me come,
And I will bear the wood for thee.
Thy well-behaved, obedient son –
On the hill this sacrifice to see.

SARAH: Hold on husband, now I pray,
For, ever as you love me dear,

Let Isaac stay with me today,
It blows so cold this time of year.

ABRAHAM: Hush, woman, and hold your tongue!
Isaac shall come with me, I say.
Do not worry for the precious one,
Soon he'll be back home to play.

SARAH: It shall be ever as you say,
But dear husband, to give me joy,
Come home as quickly as you may,
Because of Isaac, my sweet boy.

ABRAHAM: Isaac, Isaac, my darling dear,
My blessing on you I now bestow.
Take up this wood with good cheer,
For it is time that we did go.

ISAAC: Gladly, Father, this pack I bring,
And work so hard to do my part.

ABRAHAM: (*aside*)

Ah, Lord of Heaven, my hands I wring,
These childish words do break my heart!

ISAAC: I'll follow where so'er you lead,
Although I be but slender.

ABRAHAM: Ah, Lord, my heart will break indeed,
This boy's words be so tender.

(*They go to the hillside.*)

Now we have reached the place at last,
Set down thy load upon the ground.
Here sacrifice and pray as asked,
And honour God as I am bound.

ISAAC: Dear Father, here I cast it down,
But sir, that now I see thee near,
Upon your face I see a frown,
And in your eyes a look of fear.

And neither can I understand,
Why we have brought no beast to kill?

Both fire and wood we have at hand
But nothing lives upon this hill.

And yet I know some living thing
To be your sacrifice must die.

ABRAHAM: The fire was all we had to bring.
A beast will come from God on high,

It will be as the Angel spake,
Trust, my son, in our dear Lord.

ISAAC: Father, I now begin to quake
To see you hold so sharp a sword.

Why is it drawn before you so?
My heart is full of fearful wonder!

ABRAHAM: (*aside*)

Ah, Father of Heaven, so I am woe,
This child breaks my heart asunder.

ISAAC: Father, Father, tell me more!
Is your sword thus drawn for me?

ABRAHAM: My son sweet, I do implore
Have peace, my heart doth break for thee.

ISAAC: Father keep not the truth from me,
I am your beloved son!

ABRAHAM: Ah Isaac, Isaac, I must kill thee!

ISAAC: Kill me Father! What have I done?

ABRAHAM: Full loath I am thy blood to spill,
But, my son, no choice have I.

ISAAC: Now, were my mother on this hill,
She would plead I should not die.
But since my mother is not here,
I plead to save me from your knife.
I crave your mercy, Father dear,
And beg you spare my life!

ABRAHAM: This sacrifice did God ordain,
To whom I my allegiance owe.

ISAAC: Is it God's will that I be slain?

ABRAHAM: Yes, Isaac, truly it is so.

ISAAC: Then you must do as God has bidden,
And carry out our Lord's command.
But from my mother keep this hidden;
Say I have gone to some other land.

ABRAHAM: Oh, Isaac, how blessed thou must be.
But what dread sacrifice to perform!
Why must I choose 'twixt God and thee?
How my heart and soul are torn!

ISAAC: Bless me now, Father, with your hand,
Before I from this life depart.

ABRAHAM: Thou dearest child in all the land
I do thee bless with all my heart!

(*He blesses and kisses him.*)

Now, Isaac, son, speak no more,
For all your words move me to tears.

ISAAC: But I have little life in store,
And I must talk to calm my fears.

ABRAHAM: Likewise, son, I am afraid –
Except I know this is God's will.

ISAAC: Then press on, do not delay,
Since only death my fears can still.

ABRAHAM: Oh! Farewell, my child so wise,
'Tis not for us to know God's ways.

ISAAC: I pray you now to hide my eyes
That I see not the sword that slays.

ABRAHAM: Alas, I must bind thy hands also
Although thou be both good and mild.

ISAAC: Dear Father, then why must you so?

ABRAHAM: In case you try to stop me, child.

(*He binds his hands.*)

54

My dear son, hereon thou must lie,
Though I would rather it were I
Whom the Lord would have to die.
Oh, God, hear this prayer, I cry!

(*He lifts him onto the altar and blindfolds him.*)

ISAAC: Let me die but with one blow;
Strike hard and quick – a stroke of worth;
Then but little pain shall I know.

ABRAHAM: So be it, sweetest child on earth.

(ABRAHAM *raises his sword – but falters.*)

Oh, Lord, my heart will not obey,
He lies here so meek and still.
O help me, Lord of Heaven, I pray;
This gentle child I cannot kill.

ISAAC: Oh, Father, why do you delay?
Why must I linger so long here?
God commands; you must obey,
For I, thy son, am weak with fear.

(ABRAHAM *goes to strike but the* ANGEL *appears and takes the sword from his hand.*)

ANGEL: I am that Angel from God sublime
That down from Heaven to thee art sent,
To thank thee in this blessed time
For keeping his commandment.

A creature stands among the briar.
So sacrifice to God that ram;
His death is not the Lord's desire.
Now, farewell, blessed Abraham.

GOD: Abraham, thy son I spare.
But look thou well; for this world's sin
Upon a hillside bleak and bare,
My son shall die, man's soul to win.

ABRAHAM: Oh Lord, great thanks I give to theel
Thou art both merciful and wise.

Dear child, arise, and come to me.
Arise, sweet child, I say, arise!

(ABRAHAM *and* ISAAC *embrace*.)

MOSES

CHARACTERS

PHARAOH

TWO COUNSELLORS

MOSES

GOD

TWO JEWS

FIVE EGYPTIANS

MOSES

(PHARAOH *in his court; he is fanned by slaves as he strides about.*)

PHARAOH: O peace, I bid that no man pass,
　　　　　 But keep the course that I command,
　　　　　 And take good heed to him that has
　　　　　 Your life entirely in his hand.
　　　　　 King Pharaoh my father was,
　　　　　 And led the lordship of this land;
　　　　　 I am his heir, all now agree,
　　　　　 Ever in his place to rule and stand.
　　　　　 All Egypt is mine own
　　　　　 To lead after my law;
　　　　　 I will my might be known
　　　　　 And honoured, as in awe.

1ST COUNSELLOR: My Lord, there are a manner of men
　　　　　 That show great power, and strength as well,
　　　　　 The Jews that live here in our land,
　　　　　 And are called the children of Israel.
　　　　　 They multiply so fast
　　　　　 That, truly, we suppose,
　　　　　 It is likely, should they last,
　　　　　 Your lordship will you lose!

PHARAOH: What devil ever may it mean
　　　　　 That they so fast increase?

1ST COUNSELLOR: They shall confound us clean
　　　　　 If sooner they not cease.
　　　　　 How they increase, full well we know,
　　　　　 They come of Joseph, Jacob's son,
　　　　　 He was a prince worthy of praise;
　　　　　 This state of things he hath begun.

PHARAOH: Fie on them, to the devil of hell!
　　　　　 Such destiny shall we not dread;
　　　　　 We shall make midwives them to spill,
　　　　　 All Hebrew sons will be born dead!

And of the others I have no awe,
Such bondage shall we to them bid
To dig and delve, bear and draw,
And do all manner of dismal deed.
Thus shall these laddies be held in law –
Their lives afflict them all full sore!

(*Exit the Court;* MOSES *enters.*)

MOSES: Great God, that all this ground began,
And governs us all in good degree,
That made me, Moses, unto man,
And saved from the bullrushes even me –
King Pharaoh, his command he sent
So that no sons should saved be.
Against his will away I went,
Thus God has shown his might in me.
Now am I here to keep
Close by Sinai's side –
The shepherd of Jethro's sheep –
Till better times I bide.

(*He sees the Burning Bush.*)

Ah, mercy, God! Mickle is thy might!   *great*
What man may of thy marvels mene?   *understand*
I see yonder a full wondrous sight,
Whereof before no sign was seen.
A bush I see yonder, burning bright,
And the leaves, behold, still fresh and green!
If it be work of worldly wight,   *person*
I will go to see this without wene.   *delay*

GOD: Moses, come not too near,
But still in that spot dwell,
And take heed me to hear –
Attend what I thee tell!

I am thy Lord, thy shoes now take
From off thy feet, 'tis holy ground.
I am the same God that sometime spake
To Abraham whom my favour found –
To Isaac and Jacob spoke I to bless,

60

And multiply and them to make
So that their seed should ne'er be less,
And now King Pharaoh
Harms their children full fast;
If I suffer him so,
Their seed should soon be past.

Go, take the message I give now
To him that them so harmed has;
Go, warn him sternly, tell him how
That he may let my people pass;
That they to the wilderness may wend
And worship me as in former days.
But, if he will not his ways amend,
His song full soon will sing my praise.

MOSES: Ah, Lord, loved be thy will,
That makes thy folk so free,
I shall tell the people,
All thou tellest me.
But, to the King, Lord, when I come,
And he ask me what is thy name,
And I stand still then, deaf and dumb,
How shall I be without blame?

GOD: I say thus, 'Ego sum qui sum'
I AM THAT I AM, the same.

MOSES: I understand this thing,
With all the might in me.

GOD: Be bold in my blessing;
Thy protection I shall be.

MOSES: Unto my friends now will I fare,
The chosen children of Israel,
To tell them comfort of their care,
And of the danger wherein they dwell.

(*He goes to the* JEWS.)

God maintain you evermore,
Much mirth may you have in store!

61

1ST JEW: Ah, Moses, master dear,
　　　　　Our mirth is all mourning;
　　　　　We are hard oppressed here
　　　　　As slaves under the king.

MOSES: I shall carp to the king　　　　　　　　*speak*
　　　　　And try to make you free.

2ND JEW: God send us good tidings,
　　　　　All blessings with you be.

(*Enter* PHARAOH *and* COURT; MOSES *approaches.*)

MOSES: King Pharaoh, to me take tent!　　　　　*heed*

PHARAOH: Why, what tidings can'st thou tell?

MOSES: From God of heaven thus am I sent
　　　　　To fetch his folk of Israel.
　　　　　To the wilderness they all must wend.

PHARAOH: Yeah, wend thou to the devil of hell!

MOSES: Then will God vengeance take
　　　　　On thee and on all of thine.

PHARAOH: Fie on thee laddie! Out of my land!
　　　　　Thy folk should be put to pine.　　　　*torture*
　　　　　Who is this wizard with his wand
　　　　　That would thus win our folk away?

1ST COUNSELLOR: It is Moses, we well warrant,
　　　　　Against all Egypt is he, aye,
　　　　　Your father great fault in him found;
　　　　　Now he will mar you if he may.

PHARAOH: Bids God me? False lurdan, thou liest!　　*fool*

MOSES: Yea, sir, he said thou would despise.
　　　　　My wand he bade by his assent
　　　　　That you should be well advised
　　　　　How it should turn to a serpent!

(*He throws down his staff and it turns into a serpent.*)

PHARAOH: Ah, dog!

MOSES: And now to a wand again!

PHARAOH: Now this is a subtle swain –
　　　　But these boys shall bide here in our power,
　　　　For all these tricks shall nothing gain,
　　　　But worse shall be each day and hour!

MOSES: God will send his vengeance soon.

　　　(*Exit* MOSES.)

　　　(*Voices are heard howling in dismay and* MESSENGERS *come
　　　rushing on.*)

1ST EGYPTIAN: Alas, alas! This land is lorne,　　　　　*lost*
　　　　On life we may no longer lende!　　　　　　　*stay*

2ND EGYPTIAN: So great mischief is made this morn
　　　　There may no medicine us amend!

1ST COUNSELLOR: Sir King, we curse that we were born
　　　　Our bliss is all with bales blend!　　　　　*sorrows*

PHARAOH: Why cry you so, laddies?

1ST EGYPTIAN: Sir King, our water that was ordained
　　　　To men and beasts as food,
　　　　Throughout all Egypt's golden land
　　　　Is foully tuned to blood.

3RD EGYPTIAN: Lord, great maggots, both morn and noon
　　　　Bite us full bitterly!
　　　　And we see that all is done
　　　　By Moses, our enemy.

4TH EGYPTIAN: Lord, alas! Surely we die!
　　　　We dare not look out of our door.

PHARAOH: What the devil ails you so to cry?

4TH EGYPTIAN: We fare now worse than ever we were.
　　　　Great fleas over all this land they fly,
　　　　That with biting make much buzzing.

1ST EGYPTIAN: Lord, our beasts lie dead and dry,
　　　　On the dunghill and the moor,
　　　　Both ox, horse and ass,
　　　　Falleth dead down suddenly.

PHARAOH: Why carp? No man harm has
　　　Half so much as I!

2ND COUNSELLOR: Yea, Lord, poor men have much woe
　　　To see their cattle cast out.

PHARAOH: Go, say we give them leave to go.

(2ND EGYPTIAN *runs to* MOSES.)

2ND EGYPTIAN: Moses, my Lord gives leave
　　　Thy men for to remove.

MOSES: He must have more mischief
　　　The truth of his tales to prove!

(*Another* EGYPTIAN *runs to* PHARAOH.)

5TH EGYPTIAN: Wild worms are laid over all this 　　*locusts*
　　　land,
　　　They leave no fruit nor flower on tree.
　　　Against that storm may nothing stand.

3RD EGYPTIAN: Lord, there is more mischief, think me,
　　　For three days has it been dark.
　　　So mirk that none might other see.

PHARAOH: (*Storming out*)

　　　Go, say we grant them leave to be gone!

(MOSES *re-enters and gathers the* JEWS *around him.*)

MOSES: My friends, at our will now shall we wend
　　　Into a land of our liking, our days to spend.

1ST JEW: King Pharaoh, that most wicked fiend,
　　　Will feel great wrath at this our end.

MOSES: Be not afeard, God is your friend;
　　　From all our foes he will defend.
　　　Close in friendship now we stand.
　　　The Red Sea is right near at hand.

(*The Red Sea parts and* MOSES *leads his people across.*)

(PHARAOH *enters on horseback.*)

64

PHAROAH: Horse harness tight, that they be ta'en!
This riot they shall rue.
We shall not cease till they are slain.

(*leading a charge of Hobby Horses,*)

Heave up your hearts to Mahommet!
He will be near us in our need.

(*They plunge into the sea and are overwhelmed.*)

EGYPTIANS: Out, harrow! The devil, I drown!
Alas, we die for our deeds!

MOSES: Now we are won from war and saved out of the
sea,
Let us sing to the Lord, to God a song sing we!

(*They sing and dance.*)

THE LAW

CHARACTERS

GOD

MOSES

EXPOSITOR

THE LAW

(*Enter* MOSES.)

GOD: Moses, my servant beloved and dear,
And all the people that be here,
Know well, in Egypt when you were,
Out of bondage I you brought.
I will you honour no God save me,
No images nor idols now make ye,
My name in vain take not ye,
For that me liketh naught.

I will you hold your holy day;
And worship also, by all way,
Father and mother, all that you may;
And slay no man nowhere.
Fornication shall you flee;
No man's goods steal ye,
Nor in no place look ye
False witness for to bear.

Your neighbour's wives covet nought,
Servants, nor goods that he has bought,
Ox nor ass, in deed or thought,
Nor anything that is his.

In all this do my bidding
That you nothing do amiss.

(MOSES *approaches the Jews. Among them is an* EXPOSITOR
who addresses the audience.)

MOSES: You, God's folk, be you intent
To hear the Lord's commandment:
Six days boldly work you all,
The seventh Sabaoth you shall call;
That day, for ought that may befall,
Hallowed shall be alway.

EXPOSITOR: Lordings, this commandment
Was of the Old Testament.

But this story, if all of it we show
Would take far too long we know!
Wherefore, most fruitful here below
To take it now as seen!

Also we read in this story
God, in the Mount of Sinai
Gave Moses these commandments verily,
Written with His own hand,
In tables of stone, as read I;
But, when man honoured idolatry,
He brake them in anger hastily,
For that He would not stand.

But afterward, soon, believe you me
Other tablets of stone made He,
That the law be written in men's hearts
Evermore . . .

But now, behold king Balak,
And the story of Balaam – and divers prophets ye shall
   see.

BALAAM, BALAK
AND THE PROPHETS

CHARACTERS

KING BALAK

KNIGHT

BALAAM

GOD

ASS

ANGEL

ISAIAH

EXPOSITOR

MICAH

BALAAM, BALAK AND THE PROPHETS

KING BALAK: I, Balak, king of Moab land,
Am assailed by Israelites on every hand.
Their God helps them faithfully
O'er other lands to have mastery.
So it is pointless, utterly,
Against them for to fight.

KNIGHT: Whoso Balaam blesses iwis,   *indeed*
Blessed surely that man is.
Whoso he curses, fareth amiss.
Such power over all he hath.

BALAK: Balaam, I will, shall come to me
That people for to curse.

Therefore, go fetch him, bachelor,   *knight*
For that he may curse the people here.

(KNIGHT *goes to* BALAAM *who is walking alone.*)

KNIGHT: Balaam, my lord greets well thee
And prays thee right soon at his side to be,
To curse the people of Jewry
That do him great annoy.

BALAAM: Forsooth, I tell thee, bachelor,
That I may have no power
Unless God's will it were.
Then I would quickly go.

GOD: Balaam, I command thee,
From Balak's bidding thou shalt flee.
That people that is blessed of me
Curse thou not by no way!

BALAAM: Lord, I must do thy bidding,

(*aside*)

Though it be much to my unliking,
For truly, much winning

73

I might have had today.

GOD: Though the Moabites be my foe
Thou shalt have leave thither to go.
But look that you do right so
As I have thee taught.

BALAAM: Lord, it shall be done tonight;
This ass shall bear me aright,
Go we together anon, sir knight!

(*He mounts the ass.*)

(*To audience*)

Now, by the law I believe upon,
Since I have leave to be gone,
They shall be cursed every one,

(*laughs*)

If by doing thus I gain!

(*They move along but suddenly an* ANGEL *appears with a drawn sword. The ass stops and* BALAAM *is thrown off. He climbs back on and attempts to get it going.*)

Go forth, Burnell! Go forth, go!
What the devil! My ass will not go!
Served me she never so!
What sorrow so is nearby?
Rise up, Burnell, be ready boun   *prepared*
And help to bear me out of town.
Or, as I broke my crown,
Thou shalt full sore abye.

(*He beats the ass.*)

ASS: Master, thou dost evil utterly,
So good an ass to harm as I.
Now hast thou beaten me thrice
That bear you thus about.

BALAAM: Burnell, why beguil'st thou me
When I have most need of thee?

ASS: That sight that I before me see
Maketh me to bow the knee.
Am I not, master, thine own ass,
That ever before ready was
To bear thee wherever thou wouldest pass?
To smite me now it is a shame,
Thou wottest well, master, pardy,   *know*
Thou haddest never ass like to me,
Yet never thus served I thee;
Now I am not to blame.

(BALAAM *now sees the* ANGEL.)

BALAAM: Ah, Lord, to thee I make a vow!
I had no sight of thee ere now;
Little wist I it was thou   *knew*
That scared my poor ass so.

ANGEL: Why hast thou beaten thy ass thrice?
Now I am come with this advice;
You changed your purpose falsely now
And wouldest be my foe.

Had the ass not down gone,
I would have slain thee here anon.

BALAAM: Lord, have pity me upon,
For I have sinned full sore.
Is it thy will that I forth go?

ANGEL: Yea, but look thou dost His folk no woe,
Otherwise than God bade thee to
And said to thee before.

(BALAAM *and the* KNIGHT *go on their way and* BALAK *comes to meet them.*)

BALAK: Ah, welcome, Balaam, my friend!
Now all mine anguish thou shalt end
And rid me of my foe.

(BALAAM *goes to speak.*)

Come forth Balaam, come with me!
For on this hill I tell thee,

The folk of Israel thou shalt see,
And curse them, I thee pray.
Thou shalt have riches, gold and fee,
And I shall advance thy dignity.

(*He leads him to face the south.*)

Lo, Balaam, now thou seest here,
God's people all in fear,
City, castle and river,
Look now, how likes this thee?

BALAAM: How may I curse them in this place?
The people that God blessed has
In them is both might and grace.

BALAK: What the Devil ails thee, poplart,   *hypocrite*
Thy speech is not worth a fart.
To this north side thou shalt anon,
I bid thee curse them every one.

BALAAM: Hearken, Balak what I say.
God may not jib by no way.
To Jacob's blood and Israel
God shall send all joy and heal.

BALAK: Out, alas, thou preachest as a pie,   *magpie*
Thou blessest mine enemies here nearby.

BALAAM: Now, one thing I will tell you all,
Hereafter what shall befall.
A star of Jacob spring up shall,
A man of Israel.
He shall overcome and have in band
All kings, dukes of strange land,
And all the world have in his hand.
Hear what the prophets tell!
Isaiah near doth stand.

(ISAIAH *and other prophets appear.*)

ISAIAH: I say a maiden meek and mild
Shall conceive and bear a child,
And be called Emanuel.

76

EXPOSITOR: Lordings, these words are so veray,   *true*
  That exposition in good faye   *faith*
  None needs, but you know may
  This word Emanuel –
  Emanuel is as much to say
  As 'God is with us night and day'.
  Therefore, that name for ever and aye
  To his son accords wondrous well.

MICAH: I, Micah, through my mind,
  Will say that man shall surely find
  That a child of kingly kind
  In Bethlem shall be born.
  He shall rule the human race
  And win mankind e'en back to grace.
  That through Adam was lorne.   *lost*

EXPOSITOR: Lordings, much more matter
  Is in this story than you see here,
  But the substance, never fear,
  Is played you beforne;
  And by these prophesies, believe you me,
  Three kings, as you shall played see,
  Presented, at his Nativity,
  Christ when he was born.

 (*All turn except* BALAK.)

BALAK: Go we forth – it is no boot
  Longer with these men to moot,
  For God of the Jews is crop and root
  And lord of heaven and hell.
  Now I see no man alive
  Against him may hope to strive.
  Therefore, here, as I must thrive,
  I will no longer dwell.

THE ANNUNCIATION

CHARACTERS

GOD
GABRIEL
MARY
JOSEPH
SUSANNAH
CITIZEN

THE ANNUNCIATION

GOD: Good Angel Gabriel, from me go hence
Unto the land of Galilee.
At Nazareth, there find a wench.
Wedded to an ancient man is she.
His name is Joseph, and of David's line.
Here is Mary, that maid so fine.

GABRIEL: My Lord, I go.

(GABRIEL *appears to* MARY *who is discovered with two other women, both older than she, one heavily pregnant.*)

MARY: Almighty Father and King of bliss,
My mind misgives some consequence.
For inly my spirit troubled is.
God grant me now your providence.,

GABRIEL: Hail, Mary, full of grace,
Our Lord God is now with thee!
Above all women in this place,
Lady, blessed more thou be.

Thou shalt conceive upon this ground
The second of God's Trinity.
He shall be born of thee alone.

MARY: Why I?

GABRIEL: For thy virginity.

MARY: I marvel now how that may be,
For man's company knew I never yet,
Nor never will I tempted be
While God has granted me my wit.   *understanding*

GABRIEL: This child that of thee shall be born
By name of Jesus shall he be,
He shall save what was forlorn
And the Fiend's power destroy shall he.

Know well these words, full true are they;

81

And, further, maid, in thine own line,
Behold Elizabeth, thy cousin grey,
Is now with child full past her time.

MARY: Aye, she that was barren all her life,
Six months or more great grown is she.
Is this God's work? Did He contrive?

GABRIEL: To God impossible nothing may be.
Oh, thou whose sweetness cannot cloy,
Arise and take His blessing.

(MARY *rises and closes her eyes.* GOD *enters and with His hand touches her forehead. He goes.*)

MARY: I cannot tell what joy
I feel now in my body.
Gentle Gabriel, I thank you for this,
Meekly commend me to our Father.

GABRIEL: I will, my Lady, give him this kiss;
Farewell, sweet maid, our Holy Mother.

(GABRIEL *goes,* MARY *returns to the women.* JOSEPH *enters.*)

JOSEPH: Ho! Dame ho! Undo thy door!
Are ye at home? My feet are sore.

SUSANNAH: Who is there? Who cry'st so in the night?
Forbear! Thou givs't to us a fright.

JOSEPH: Undo thy door,
I say to you,
For to 'come in'
These cries construe.

MARY: Ah, it is my spouse that speaks't to us,
Undo the door as he bids thus.

(ELIZABETH *goes to* JOSEPH, *bids him enter.* JOSEPH *pats her stomach.*)

Welcome home, mine husband dear,
How hast thou fared in that far country?

JOSEPH: I've laboured long for most a year.

Thy face, my wife, is changed brightly.

(MARY *rises and reveals her pregnancy.*)

Ye be with child!
I've been deceived! My honour shent!   disgraced
Say woman, who hath been here since I went?

MARY: Sir, here was neither man, nor man's even,
But only the word of our Lord of heaven.

JOSEPH: Say not so, woman; for shame, let be!
This child's not mine, alas for me.
Tell me woman whose is this child?

MARY: None but yours, my husband mild.

JOSEPH: Let all old men example take.
See, I am disgraced, 'twas my mistake
To wed a fair and pretty maid.
Farewell my love, I'm rightly paid.

MARY: Nay, truly, sir, ye be not beguiled
Nor yet with sin am I defiled.
An angel brought God's holy son
And of your wife he shall be born.

JOSEPH: An angel! An angel! Alas, now, for thy shame
To put an angel in such blame!
Were it not so sad, 'twould make me laugh.
Now farewell Mary, my better half!

(JOSEPH *withdraws.*)

MARY: God, that in my body art seized,
Thou knowest my husband is displeased
To see me in this plight.
Oh, send a word by Gabriel,
So he will know what has befell,
And put his mind to right.

(GABRIEL *appears to* JOSEPH, *who weeps.*)

GABRIEL: Joseph, Joseph, why weepest thou?

JOSEPH: Why, for my wife, whom I didst love.

GABRIEL: As God did, and still does now,
Thus He commands thee from above.

(JOSEPH *looks at* GABRIEL.)

I am the angel that God did send.
Now go to Mary and comfort her,
And to her thou shoulds't make amend
For she is pure as was before.

JOSEPH: O, Lord, I thank thee with all my heart,
For of these tidings I am so glad.
I'll straight to Mary now depart
And no more think why I was sad.

(*He returns to* MARY.)

Ah Mary, Mary, I kneel full low,
Forgive me, sweet wife; here, in this land,
Mercy, Mary, for now I know
Of your good grace, and how it doth stand.

And now to Bethlehem must I wend   *go*
To make an Emperor's tribute there.
Am I to leave you, thus great, behind?
Tell me, Mary, how you should fare.

MARY: Nay, hardily, husband, dread ye nothing,   *certainly*
For I will ride there all the way.
I trust in God, our mighty King,
To speed us on our journey.

(JOSEPH *helps* MARY *mount a donkey. He picks up his belongings.*)

JOSEPH: I thank ye, Mary, for your goodness
That for my words ye did not blame.
So to Bethlehem we shall us dress.
Go we together in God's name.

(*They begin the journey.*)

MARY: Ho, Joseph, sweet husband, woulds't tell to me
What tree stands yonder on that hill?

JOSEPH: By name it is called a cherry tree,

Of that tree's fruit ye may eat thy fill.
'Tis meet we journey with all haste
To yonder city without stop.

MARY: But, husband, I crave the fruit thereof.
Please fetch me some, from the tree top.

JOSEPH: I have no time to labour thus,
To pluck the fruit that here grows wild,
For this tree grows so high o'er us.
Let him give thee cherries that gave thee child.

MARY: Good Lord I pray, grant me this boon,
Give me these cherries if 'tis thy will.

(*The tree bends down.*)

I thank thee Lord, the tree bows low,
Now I mays't eat of it my fill.

JOSEPH: Lord, mercy, again I have offended thee,
Saying to my spouse unkind words thus.
For now I know, it may none other be
But that she bears the King of Bliss.

(*They travel on and enter Bethlehem; a man stands to greet them.*)

Worshipful sir, we bid thee good day.
Of Bethlehem ye seem to be.
Knowst thou a room wherein, I pray,
I may rest, and my wife Mary?

CITIZEN: Sir, this city is so full of late,
No room, know I, will thou find here.
But try against the city gate.

JOSEPH: I will; come on my, darling dear.
Ah, sweet my wife, what shall we do?
Where shall we lodge this night?

CITIZEN: Ho, sir, I have a stable, lo,
With beasts thou mayest spend the night.

MARY: Good husband, in haste, I say to you
My time is at an end,

Let's to the stable.

JOSEPH: Kind sir, adieu.

MARY: Husband, help me descend.

(*She dismounts from the donkey and together they enter the stable.*)

Now that I am in the stable brought,
I hope, right well, my child to see.
Go from me husband, I'll need thee naught.
Go from this place and leave me be.

(JOSEPH *goes out of the stable and tends the donkey.* MARY *goes to the back of the stable and kneels amongst the straw. After a moment, she returns to the front of the stable with the Baby Jesus in her arms. The stable fills with light. Angels sing.*)

MARY: Behold the child that God hath given,
Of God the incarnate Word.
Praise we now our King in heaven,
And thee, our infant Lord.

(*They all sing a carol.*)[1]

The Passion

1. See Appendix.

THE SHEPHERDS

CHARACTERS

FIRST SHEPHERD (COLL)
SECOND SHEPHERD (GIB)
THIRD SHEPHERD (DAW)
MAK
MAK'S WIFE (GILL)
ANGEL
MARY

THE SHEPHERDS

(*Enter* FIRST SHEPHERD (COLL) *moaning and grumbling*.)

COLL: Lord, what these weathers are cold!
        And I am ill happed.
        I am nearly dold, so long have I napped;   *numb*
        My legs they fold, for I am all lapped
        In sorrow.
        In storms and tempest,
        Now in the east, now in the west,
        Woe is him has never rest
        Mid-day nor morrow!

        But we seely shepherds that walk on the moor, *wretched*
        In faith, we are almost out of the door.
        No wonder as it stands, if we be poor,
        For the tilth of our lands lies fallow as the floor
        As you know;
        We are so crippled,
        Over-taxed and crushed,
        We are made hand-tamed
        By these gentry-men.

        It does me good, as I walk thus by mine own,
        Of this world to talk in manner of moan.   *grumbling*
        To my sheep will I stalk and harken anon,
        There abide on a balk or sit on a stone.
        Full soon,
        For I trow, pardy,   *by God*
        True men if they be,
        We get more company
        Ere it be noon.

(*Enter* SECOND SHEPHERD (GIB) *who does not see* COLL.
COLL *tries to attract his attention and communicates his
amusement to the audience*.)

GIB: Benste and Dominus, what may this mean?
        Why fares this world thus? Oft have we not seen.

91

Lord, these weathers are spitous, and the winds   *cruel*
    full keen,

And the frosts so hideous they water mine een –   *eyes*
No lie.
Now in dry, now in wet,
Now in snow, now in sleet,
When my shoon freeze to my feet
It is not all easy.

But as far as I ken, or yet as I go,
We married men endure much woe –
We have sorrow then and then; it falls out so.
Silly Copple, our hen, both to and fro
She cackles;
But begin she to croak,
To groan or to cluck,
Woe is him our cock,
For he is in the shackles.

But, as ever I read epistle, I have my wife to fear,
As sharp as a thistle, as rough as a briar.
She has brows like a bristle, and a sour face to cheer;
And once she wets her whistle, she can sing full clear
Her paternoster.
She is as great as a whale,
And most hearty and hale,
But, by my cup of ale,
I would to God I had lost her!

(COLL *tries to whistle to gain his attention.*)

COLL: Lord help our audience the more! Deaf as a post you
    stand.

GIB: (*Surprised.*)

Oh, the devil in your maw, how was this planned!

(*Recovering his composure.*)

Saw'st thou ought of Daw?

COLL: Yes, on the lea-land

I heard him blow. He comes here at hand,
Not far.
Stand still!

GIB: Why?

COLL: For he comes, hope I.

(*Sound of horn and they hide.*)

(*Enter* THIRD SHEPHERD (DAW).)

DAW: Was never since Noah's flood such floods seen,
Winds and rains so rude, and storms so keen:
Some men stammer, some stand in doubt, as I have
    seen,
Now God turn all to good: I say as I mean.
For ponder –
These floods, so they drown,
Both in fields and in town
And bear all down;
And that is a wonder.

We that walk in the nights, our cattle to keep,
We see sudden sights when other men sleep.

(*He sees the other shepherds peeping out.*)

Yet methink my heart lights; I see shrews peep.
Ye are two monsters!
Sir, God save you, and master mine!
A drink fain would I have, and somewhat to dine!

(GIB *and* COLL *leap at him and roll him over – good
humouredly.*)

GIB: Well, boy, sit we down all three and drink shall we
    then.

COLL: Yea, Gib, but I would rather eat,
What is drink without meat?
Lay forth of our store.

DAW: Set mustard afore,
Our meal now begins.

(They each produce items from their bags.)

GIB: Here a foot of a cow,
       Well soused I wene.   *think*
       The leg of a sow,
       That pickled has been.

COLL: Two blood puddings I trow,
       A liver sausage between.

DAW: Do gladly, sirs, now my bread begin,
       With more;
       Both beef and mutton
       Of a ewe that was rotten,

COLL: Good meat for a glutton,
       Now eat of this store.

       I have here soused in ale, boiled and roast
       Even an ox tail.
       Onion, garlick, juicy leeks,
       And green cheese that will grease your cheeks.

DAW: Now reach us a drink –
       This food hath given me a thirst;
       So shall we drink of this good brew.
       Come! Wet your mouths; Gib, be thou first.
       Good wholesome ale gives life anew!

       (They drink.)

GIB: In faith, by the rood, these nights are long,
       Yet, I would ere we went that we sing a song.

COLL: So I thought as I stood, to mirth us among.

DAW: I grant.

GIB: Let me sing the tenor,

DAW: And I the treble so high,

COLL: Then the bass falls to me.
       Let's hear how you chant!

       (They sing.)

       Of every kind of tree,

Of every kind of tree,
The hawthorn blows the sweetest
Of every kind of tree.

My lover she shall be,
My lover she shall be,
Of earthly girls the fairest
My lover she shall be.[1]

(**MAK** *enters with a cloak covering his smart tunic – he has acquired a livery and 'southern' airs and graces. He tries to join in the singing.*)

GIB: Who is that that pipes so poor?

COLL: Mak! Where hast thou been?

DAW: Is he come? Then all take heed to this thing!

(*They pull off* **MAK**'s *cloak and laugh.*)

MAK: I am all uneven.
I be a yeoman, I tell you, of the king;
The self and the same, messenger of a great lording,
And such like.
Fie on you! Go hence
Out of my presence!
I must have reverence.

GIB: Mak, why are you so quaint? Mak, you do wrong.

DAW: Mak, playing the saint! Sing another song.

MAK: I shall make complaint, and have you flogged at a
word.

COLL: Now take out that southern tooth,
And set in a turd!

MAK: I am true as steel, as all men wot;   *know*
But a sickness I feel that holds me full hot:
My belly fares not well, it is out of estate.   *condition*

COLL: Seldom lies the devil dead by the gate.

MAK: Therefore, full sore am I and ill:
If I stand stone-still,

1. See Appendix.

I eat not a needle   *morsel*
This month and more.

GIB: How fares thy wife? By my hood, how fares she?

MAK: Lies sprawling – by the rood – by the fire, lo!
        And a house full of brood. She drinks well too;
        She eats as fast as she can,
        And each year that comes to a man
        She brings forth a baby,
        And, some years, two!

GIB: Mak, come hither! Between shalt thou lie.
        We are weary and cold and want for a fire,
        Naked, worn out with walking in mire.

(*They lie down to sleep while* MAK *still sits.*)

MAK: From my top to my toe
        'Manus tuas commendo,
        Pontio Pilato.'
        Christ's cross me speed!

(*Pretends to sleep and after a while he tiptoes away.*)

MAK: Now were a time for a man that lacks what he
            would,
        To stalk privily unto a fold . . .
        But about you a circle, as round as a moon,

(*He circles them.*)

        Till I have done what I will, till that it be noon
        That ye lie stone-still, till that I have done.
        Over your heads, my hand I lift.
        Out go your eyes! Forgo your sight . . .
        Lord, what they sleep hard!
        A fat sheep now tonight!

(*He makes various ludicrous attempts to catch a sheep and
eventually gets one; he goes off with it to his house. His wife,
*GILL *is spinning.*)

MAK: How, Gill, art thou in? Get us some light.

WIFE: Who makes such din at this time of the night?

I am set for to spin.

MAK: Good wife, open the door! See'st thou not what I
       bring?

WIFE: Why not say 'twas thee before? Come in my
       sweeting!

MAK: Care you not that here without I am stand?

WIFE: (*Seeing the sheep.*)

       By the naked neck, thou art like to hang!

MAK: Come away!
       For in a night can I get
       More than they that swink and sweat   *toil*
       All the long day.
       But come and help fast,
       I would he were skinned; I am eager to eat –
       This twelve month was I not so longing for one sheep
          meat.

WIFE: Come they ere he be slain and hear the sheep bleat?

MAK: Then might I be ta'en: that were a cold sweat!
       Go bar the gate-door.

WIFE: Yes, Mak,
       For if they come at thy back
       Here shall we him hide, till they be gone,
       In my cradle. Abide! Let me alone
       And I shall lie beside in childbed and groan.

MAK: Make ready,
       And I shall say thou wast delivered right
       Of a knave-child – born this night!   *boy*

WIFE: This is a good guise and a far cast;
       Yet a woman's advice helps at the last!

MAK: I will go sleep
       With that company.
       And I shall stalk privily,
       As it had never been I
       That carried off their sheep!

(MAK *returns and lies between the shepherds.* COLL *wakes.*)

COLL: Ah . . . Have hold my hand,
My foot sleeps, I cannot stand.
In faith, I dreamt that we laid us near England.

GIB: Ah, yea?
Lord, what I have slept well,
As fresh as an eel.
As light I me feel
As leaf on tree.

DAW: See you where Mak is now?
I dreamed he was lapped in a wolf skin.

GIB: He is here.
Rise Mak, for shame! Thou liest right long.

MAK: Now Christ's holy name be us among!
What is this? Ah, my neck has lain wrong.
I thought Gill began to croak and travail full   *labour*
    sad   *hard*
Well-nigh at the first cock of a young lad.
I must go home, by your leave, to Gill, as I thought.
I pray you look my sleeve, that I steal nought.

(*He runs off.*)

COLL: Go forth!
Now would I we sought, this morn,
That we have all our store.

GIB: And I will go before.

DAW: Then let us meet.

GIB: Where?

COLL: At the crooked thorn.

(*They count the sheep.*)

GIB: Alas, that ever I was born! We are tempest tossed –
A fat sheep we have lost.

COLL: Marry, God forbid!

DAW: Who should do us that scorn?

GIB: I have sought with my dogs
All Rough Common shrogs   *bushes*
And, of fifteen hogs,
Found I but one ewe.

DAW: Now believe me, if you will – by Saint Thomas of
Kent,
Either Mak or Gill made it their intent.

COLL: Peace man, be still! I saw where he went.
Thou slanderest him ill; thou ought to repent.

GIB: Now I should even here die,
I would say it were he.

DAW: Go we thither, I advise, and run on our feet,
Nor never eat bread, till with him we meet.

(*Exeunt the shepherds, running.* MAK *enters his cottage,
running.*)

MAK: Undo this door! Who is there? How long shall I
stand?

WIFE: Who makes such a din? Come in, by this hand!

MAK: Ah, Gill what cheer? It is I, Mak, your husband.

WIFE: What end hast thou made with the herds, Mak?

MAK: The last word that they said when I turned my back,
They would look that they had their sheep, all the pack.

WIFE: Hearken when they call, for they will come anon.
Come and make ready all, and sing by thine own.

(*She organises him while he panics – the sheep is put in the
cradle and she sits in a chair.* MAK *starts to sing and* GILL
groans. The SHEPHERDS *enter.*)

DAW: Will ye hear how they hack! Our gentleman begins
to croon.

COLL: Heard I never none crack so much out of tune.   *bawl*
Call on him.

GIB: Mak, undo your door soon!

MAK: Who is it that spake, as if it were noon.
Who is that, I say?

GIB: 'Tis your fellows.

MAK: (*Opening the door – they push in past him.*)

Ye have run in the mire, and are wet yet;
I shall make you a fire, if ye will sit.
A nurse would I hire.
I would ye dined ere ye go. . . .

COLL: Nay, neither mends our mood drink nor meat.

MAK: Why, sir, ails you ought but good?

DAW: Yea, our sheep that we tend are stolen,
Our loss is great.

COLL: Mak, some men believe that it should be ye.

DAW: Either ye or your spouse, so say we.

MAK: Now if ye have suspicion of Gill or me,
Come and rip our house, and then may ye see.

(*They all start to search.*)

WIFE: Ah, my middle!
I pray to God so mild,
If ever I you beguiled,
That I may eat this child
That lies in the cradle.

MAK: Peace woman, for God's pain, and cry not so,
Thou spillest thy brain, and makest me full woe.   *hurt*

GIB: I think our sheep be slain. What find ye two?

COLL: All work we in vain; as well may we go.

DAW: (*To* MAK)

Is your child a knave?

MAK: Aye, when he wakens, he smiles that joy is to see.

COLL: Mak, friends will we be, for we must agree
In all things.

The Shepherds

(*The* SHEPHERDS *depart;* MAK *sits down with exhaustion and relief;* GILL *laughs.*)

COLL: (*On the way home.*)

Gave ye the child anything?

GIB: I trow not one farthing.   *declare*

DAW: Back we must go to remedy this thing.

(*They return and hammer on the door.*)

Mak, take it to no grief if I come to thy bairn.

GIB: Mak, with your leave, let me give your bairn
But sixpence.

MAK: Nay, get away! He sleeps.

GIB: Methinks he peeps.

MAK: When he wakens he weeps.
I pray you go hence.

(*They press round the cradle.*)

GIB: Give me leave him to kiss, and lift up the clout.

(*Sees the sheep*)

What the devil is this? He has a long snout!

COLL: He is misshapen, we should not pry about.

DAW: I durst say his smell comes most foully out:
He is like to our sheep.

MAK: Peace,
I am him that he begat, and yon woman him bore.

WIFE: As pretty child is he
That sits on woman's knee.

GIB: I know it by the ear mark; that is good token.

MAK: I tell you sirs, hark! His nose was broken.

WIFE: He was taken by an elf,
I saw it myself.
When the clock struck twelve,
Was he forshapen.

101

GIB: Since they maintain their theft, let's do them dead.

MAK: If I trespass again, strike off my head!

COLL: For this trespass
We will neither quarrel nor curse,
Nor make matters worse,
But cast him in canvas.

(*They toss* MAK *in a blanket and an* ANGEL *suddenly appears; sounds of 'Glory to God in the Highest'. There is a blinding light.*)

ANGEL: Rise, gentle herdsmen, for now is he born
That shall take from the fiend that Adam had
   lorne,
That warlock to kill, this night is he born.
God is made your friend now at this morn.
He behests.
At Bethlehem go see
Where lieth he
In a crib full poorly,
Betwixt two beasts.

(COLL *sings.*)

GIB: To Bethlehem he bade us we should gang,   *go*
I am full afraid that we tarry too long.

DAW: Be merry, not sad, of mirth is our song.

COLL: Hie we hither therefore,
Though we be wet and weary,
To that child and that lady
There to bend the knee before.

(*They move towards Bethlehen.*)

GIB: We find by the prophecy – let be your din! –
Of David and Isaiah, and more than I min –   *remember*
They prophesied by clergy – that in a virgin   *learning*
Should he descend and lie, to quench our sin,
And slake it,   *relieve*
Our kind, from woe;   *race*

For Isaiah said so.
Behold a virgin shall conceive
And bear a child.

DAW: Full glad may we be, and abide that day
That lovely to see, that all mights may.
Lord, well were me for once and for aye,
Might I kneel on my knee, some word for to say
To that child.
But the angel said
In a crib was he laid;
He was poorly arrayed,
Both meek and mild.

COLL: When I see him and feel,
Then I shall know full well
It is as true as steel
That prophets have spoken,
To so poor as we he would appear!

GIB: Go we now – the place is near,
I hear the virgin sing.

(*They approach the stable with tentative steps.* MARY *sings a cradle song*[1] *and* JOSEPH *greets them.*)

COLL: Hail, comely and clean; hail young child!
Hail, my maker, born of a maiden so mild!
Thou hast cursed, I ween, the warlock so   *know*
   wild,
The false guiler, I mean; now goes he beguiled.
Lo, he merries,
Lo, he laughs, my sweeting!
A full fair meeting.
I bring thee my greeting:
Have a bob of cherries.

GIB: Hail, sovereign saviour, for thou hast us sought!
Hail, freely food and flower, that all thing   *fair child*
   hast wrought!
Hail, full of favour, that made all of nought!

1. See Appendix.

Hail! I kneel and I cower. A bird have I brought
To my bairn.
Hail, little tiny mop!   *moppet*
Of our creed thou art crop;
I would drink on thy cop,
Little day-starn.

DAW: Hail, darling dear, full of Godhead!
I pray thee be near when that I have need.
Hail, sweet is thy cheer! My heart would bleed
To see thee sit here in so poor weed,   *clothing*
With no pennies.
I give thee my all,
I bring thee but a ball:
Have and play thee withal,
And go to the tennis.

MARY: The Father of heaven, God omnipotent,
That created all things, his Son has he sent,
And now is he born
To keep you from woe!
I shall pray him so.
Tell forth as ye go,
And remember this morn.

(*The* SHEPHERDS *go to* MARY, *raise her up, and process –
singing as they go.*)

HEROD AND THE SLAYING OF THE INNOCENTS

CHARACTERS

THREE KINGS
HEROD
MESSENGER
TWO COUNSELLORS
ANGEL
MARY
GOD
TWO KNIGHTS
JOSEPH
WOMEN

HEROD AND THE SLAYING OF
THE INNOCENTS

(1ST KING *enters*.)

1ST KING: Lord of everlasting life and light,
Eastwards have I travelled to this land.
For thou has let me see this sight,
And its meaning I would understand
Of yonder star that burneth bright.
For now the wondrous light stands still.
Oh, great Majesty, in all thy might,
Tell me now what is thy will?

(*Two other* KINGS *enter*.)

Good Sirs and fellow Lords, I pray
That I may know what you intend.
Why do you journey forth this way
And from what country do you wend?   *come*

2ND KING: Full gladly, Sir, I shall reply;
A sudden star was to us sent,
A royal star that rose on high
Before us in the firmament.
That star led us to this place
As if its mystery to show.

1ST KING: Dear Lord in God's good grace,
This star's meaning I would know.

3RD KING: They say that when a star shines bright,
Out of the East will rise and stand
A King strong and full of might,
Who will be Lord of every land.
It is this King that we do seek.

1ST KING: Oh dear fellows, I too have journeyed far
Although I am both old and weak.
Can we not together follow yonder star?

2ND KING: What you ask, shall be so.

Together we'll unite as one,
To seek God's favoured child we'll go
Until our holy quest is done.

3RD KING: Now fellows, this matter understand;
Let us pause and wait a while.
Sir Herod is King of this land
And famed, his nature volatile.

1ST KING: I thank you Lord, for, your wise thought.
We must engage here all our skill,
And make our way to Herod's court
To gain this King's good will.

(*The* KINGS *journey to* HEROD'S *court and are greeted by a* MESSENGER.)

MESSENGER: Herod, the high King, now you must know
Chief, Lord of Lordlings, chief leader of law.
They wait on his wings that bold boast will blow.
Great dukes all deferring now in great awe
Before bow down.
Tuscany and Turkey,
All India and Italy,
Syria and Sicily,
All dread his renown.

Here he comes now, as was you foretold.
Fast afore will I hie, running full bold,
For to welcome him worshipfully, laughing threefold.
As he is most worthy, kneel as you're told
So low.
Down dutifully fall
For rank most royal.
Hail, the worthiest of all
To thee I must bow.

(HEROD *enters.*)

HEROD: I am the cause of great light and thunder,
Before me the elements quiver and quake.
I am viewed by the world with great wonder,
To me all peoples do shiver and shake.

Behold now my attire and my complexion,
Brighter than the sun in the middle of the day.
Am I not God-like, near to perfection?
Come forward you all with your homage to pay.

MESSENGER: Sir Herod, King of great renown . . .

HEROD: Peace, dastard in the Devil's name.

MESSENGER: But I bring news that near this town . . .

HEROD: What boy! I will thee tame;
Go, beat that boy and break his back!

MESSENGER: Lord, messengers should no man smite,
My word deserves not such attack.

HEROD: Well, speak to me. Release him knight.

MESSENGER: My Lord, I heard upon this morn
Three kings together speak
Of one that is new born;
News of him here they seek.

HEROD: Three Kings, forsooth.

MESSENGER: Sir, so I say,
For I myself saw them appear.

1ST COUNSELLOR: My Lord, ask him more, we pray.

HEROD: Say, fellow, are they far or near?

MESSENGER: My lord, they will be here this day.
This is the truth and that is clear.

HEROD: Have done! Dress us in rich array.
And every man make merry cheer,
That nothing may be seen
But friendship and good will,
Till we know what they mean;
Whether it be good or ill.

(*The* KINGS *approach* HEROD.)

1ST KING: The Lord who sends us holy light,
And has led us from our land,

109

Keep thee, Sir King and comely knight,
And these folk here at hand.

HEROD: May Mohamet, my god, full of might,
Who from his heaven guides all things,
Keep you, good sirs, goodly in his sight.
What is your mission here, Sir Kings?

2ND KING: In our separate lands, we all did view
A star which appeared to us one morn.
This, we hope, will lead us to
Where the child we seek is born.

HEROD: What, to find a babe? Are ye gone mad?
What silly, unwitty men are here?   *foolish*
To leave their lands to find a lad?
At this nonsense I must sneer.

3RD KING: Sire, the child has been foretold,
A king to rule Jewry and other land.
For it is written in our books of old,
This is God's will and His command.

HEROD: A King! The devil take you! Fie!
Now I see well how you rant and rave.
How can a shimmering in the sky,
Show where is such king or knave?
Nay, I am King and none but I
Have power in this land to spoil or save.

2ND COUNSELLOR: (*aside*)

My Lord, although these fellows do defame,
Their true purpose we should know;
And, my King, why they this way came,
So ask them more before they go.

HEROD: I thank you for your counsel plain,
Indeed it shall be so.

Now, Kings, I'll cast all care away,
So go in peace my friends so wise.
But say before you go this day,
Your reasons why this babe you prize.

1ST KING: Balaam foretold a star should spring
From the Jews, Jacob's kith and kin.

2ND KING: Isaiah, that a maid would bring
A new born babe, full free from sin,

3RD KING: That of all countries would be King
And the world's honour win.

HEROD: (*aside*)

Alas, then I am lost for sure,
And threatened all about.

1ST COUNSELLOR: My Lord Herod, fear no more,
Let these men leave without a doubt,
But say they should return to you
Once they have this baby found.

HEROD: Your counsel again is good and true,
With my cunning I shall astound.

(*To the three* KINGS)

Now go your way, but I beg one thing,
That once the babe is found, that you
Come back this way with news to bring,
So I may go and worship too.

2ND KING: Sir, we shall do as you say
And tell you of this child.
We shall return here, come what may.

2ND COUNSELLOR: Farewell, you are beguiled.

(KINGS *exit.*)

HEROD: For sure this is a subtle scheme.
I send these fellows on the quest
To find the babe of which they dream;
When they return their wit I will test.
If this be true, I'll make them scream.
They shall be slain at my behest!

(HEROD *exits and the three* KINGS *re-enter, seemingly lost.*)

1ST KING: Ah sirs, we have followed far.

111

Where is our sign, our guiding light?

2ND KING: No longer shines our bright star
Before us in the winter night.

3RD KING: Oh sirs, behold, I see it stand
Above the place where he is born.
Lo! the house is here at hand.
Blessed be this holy morn!

(ANGEL *leads them to the stable.*)

Come forth, good sirs, and see
The place you are brought.
Behold before you, Kings all three,
The wondrous sight that you have sought.

(*One by one, the* KINGS *go forward to present their gifts.*)

1ST KING: Hail, Lord that all this world hath wrought!
Hail, God and man together in one!
For thou hast made all things of nought,
Though humbly thou liest here, God's son.
A cup of gold have I thee brought,
Thy holy will on earth be done.

2ND KING: Hail to Thee, Lord of magnificence,
For thy dignity and priesthood!
To thee, I offer a cup of incense,
For thy sacrifice, our Heavenly Food.

3RD KING: Hail be thou, Lord that we longed for!
My gift is myrrh for thy mortality.
In coming, thou shalt mankind restore
To life by thy death upon a tree.

MARY: Sirs, ye have not been deceived,
For ye have found what you did seek.
My child was from God conceived,
Though born in such a place and weak.
He is God's Holy Son perceived,
Born to the world a baby meek.

(MARY *and* JESUS *withdraw.*)

112

2ND KING: Let us now to King Herod go,
            So that he may find this place,
            And gladly kneel also
            Before the King of every race.

1ST KING: First let us rest, for need
            We surely have of sleep.
            Then unto Herod's court speed
            Our promise there to keep.

(KINGS *lie down and sleep and* GOD *and* ANGEL *appears.*)

GOD: Herod the King on your murder is bent;
       For he with envy plans your end,
       So, to save you from his cruel intent,
       'Tis my will another way home ye wend.

(KINGS *flee*.)

(HEROD *enters with his court of* KNIGHTS *and* COUNSELLORS.)

HEROD: Why have they passed me by? Give breath I gasp!
         Oh Fie!
         Fie on the devil! Where can I bide
         Unless I fight and terribly chide?
         Scoundrels, I say ye should have spied
         And told when they went by!

(HEROD *goes round hitting the* KNIGHTS *in a fury.*)

Are you Knights to trust? Nay you are louts and thieves!
I will yield up my ghost, so sore my heart it grieves.

1ST KNIGHT: Why need you be so aghast? There are no great
              mischiefs
              To make your teeth gnash.

2ND KNIGHT: Why make ye such reproofs?
              Please, please thou shouldst not threaten us,
              And ungainly beat us.
              You should not rebuke us
              Without full cause.

113

HEROD: Fie, loggerheads and liars! Lazy louts each one!
Traitors and much worse! Knaves, but Knights none!
Had ye been more diligent, they would not have gone.
I'll get those vagabonds, I'll break their every bone.
My retaliation
Will be their crying moans,
And see their rotting bones,
To pelt them with such stones,
Yes, their mutilation!

Counsellors, tell me quickly what ye find?

1ST COUNSELLOR: Truly sir, prophecy it is not blind.
We read by Isaiah, he shall be so king,
That a maiden, sweetly, who has never sinned
Shall him bear,
And him shall honour
Both King and Emperor.

HEROD: Why and should I to him cower?
Nay, should I scare?

Heard I never such a truth, that a knave so slight
Should come like the meek and rob me of my right.
Nay, his body shall creak; I shall cut him down in spite!
Ever, I say, will I him seek. I am ready for to fight.
Fie knaves!
Fie dottypolls, with your books,
Go cast them in the brooks!
With such wiles and crooks,
My wit away raves.

Should a child in a cave, but one year of age,
Thus make me rave?

2ND COUNSELLOR: Sir, quieten this outrage!
Away let ye rave all such language,
Your worship to save, for he is nought but a page
Of one year.
We two shall be so keen,
With our wits between.
If ye do just as I mean
He shall die on a spear.

114

1ST COUNSELLOR: For dread that he reign, by us now be
        dead.
    Throughout Bethlehem and every other stead   *place*
    Give knights orders to put unto dead
    All knave-children of two years' bed.
    For, by this way,
    The child's blood may ye spill
    Thus, at your own will.

HEROD: What you suggests doth me thrill;
    It shall be as you say.
    Knights! To Bethlehem you must go and all the coast
        around,
    All knave-children for to slay. Let my terror now
        abound!
    Of years if they be two or less, they must be found.
    Leave none alive my purpose to confound.
    I command you
    Spare no kin's blood.
    Let all run in a flood!
    Crush all babyhood
    And do it swiftly too!

(HEROD *and* COURT *exit.* GOD *appears to the sleeping*
JOSEPH.)

GOD: Awake, Joseph, and prepare!
    Arise and sleep no more.
    Move quickly if thou hast a care.
    Leave this place with haste, for
    I, The Lord, this word hath sent
    To warn you of impending doom.
    Now is the time that you all went
    Into Egypt from this gloom,
    For danger here is near at hand.
    Take now your wife and babe and flee
    And swiftly leave this land,
    For this, I say, my decree.

JOSEPH: I thank thee, Lord, for this thy word
    That tells us of the dangers nigh.
    Your warning I have fully heard,

And so to Egypt we will fly.

(MARY *and* JOSEPH *and the child exit.*)

(*Enter a group of women with their babes. They sing the Coventry Carol.*)

WOMEN: Lully, lullay, thou little tiny child.
By, By. Lully, lullay.
Thy poor youngling,
To whom we do sing
By, By. Lully, lullay.

Herod the King in his raging,
Charged he hath this day
His men of might,
In his own sight,
All young children to slay.

(*They repeat the first verse and during this the* SOLDIERS *enter and slay the babies.*)

(GOD *appears to the Holy Family in Egypt.*)

GOD: Arise, Joseph! Have no more dread
Of Herod's might, for he is dead.
A homeward path you now can tread
That leads unto Judea.
No more the cruel Herod reigns
Who sought to have your Jesu slain.
Take him and Mary home again
And live no more in fear.

JOHN THE BAPTIST

CHARACTERS

JOHN
JESUS
GOD

JOHN THE BAPTIST

(*A crowd is forming by the River Jordan; the voice of* JOHN *approaching is heard.*)

JOHN: Repent ye, and be baptised!
I am a voice, crying in the wilderness,
Repent ye, and come to baptism!

(*Enter* JOHN.)

Almighty God and Lord alway,
Full wonderful is man's sinning,
For, if I preach to them day by day,
And tell them, Lord, of thy coming,
That all has wrought,
Men are so dull that my preaching
Serves of naught.

When I have, Lord, in the name of Thee,
Baptised the folk in water clear,
Then have I said that, after me,
Shall he come that has more power,
Than I entire.
He shall give baptism more complete
In spirit and fire.

Thus am I come with message right
To be fore-runner, that is certain,
In witness bearing of that light,
The which shall light on every man
That is born
Into this world: now whoever can
May understand.

(*The people come to him and he baptises them in the Jordan.*
JESUS *has now joined the people and comes forward to be
baptised.*)

Full well I know, baptism is taken
To wash and cleanse man of his sin;
And well I know that sin is none

In thee, be it without or within.
What need you then
For to be baptised more than I,
A sinful man?

JESUS: Come, baptise me, John, in this place.

JOHN: Lord, save thy grace, that I forbid
That it be so;
For, Lord, me thinketh it were more need
Thou baptised me.
That place that I yearn for most of all,
From thence come thou, Lord, as I guess;
How should I then, that is in thrall,
Give thee baptism, that righteous is,
And has been ever?
For thou art the root of righteousness,
That trespassed never.

JESUS: Thou sayest full well, John, certainly,
But suffer now, for heavenly mead,
That righteousness be not only
Fulfilled in word, but also in deed.
Now baptise me in my manhood
Openly here.

First shall I take, then shall I preach.
For so it behoves mankind to fulfill
All righteousness.

JOHN: Lord, I am ready at thy will.

(JESUS *enters the water and kneels before* JOHN.)

Jesus, my Lord of mights the most,
I baptise thee here in the name
Of the Father, and of the Son and Holy Ghost.

(*A brilliant shaft of light falls on* JESUS *and the voice of* GOD *is heard.*)

GOD: This is my beloved Son, in whom I am well pleased.

JOHN: I love thee, sovereign and healer, Lord,
That comes to soothe men of their sores.

John the Baptist

As thou commandest, I will preach thy word abroad
And teach to every man thy laws.
Man was in thrall,
But, Sirs, that babe that Mary bore
Be with you all!

THE MINISTRY: TEMPTATION AND TEACHING

CHARACTERS

JESUS

SATAN

SCRIBE

ACCUSER

PHARISEE

YOUNG MAN

WOMAN

THE MINISTRY: TEMPTATION
AND TEACHING

(JESUS *is alone in the wilderness, praying. Enter* SATAN.)

SATAN: Now, by my sovereignty, I swear,
And principality that I bear
In hell, pain, when I am there,
A jest I will assay.   *try out*
There is a dosey-beard I would smear   *muddle-head*
That walks about everywhere;
Who is his father I wot not nere,   *have no idea*
The sooth if I should say.   *truth*

What master man ever be this
That in the world thus comen is?
His mother, I wot, did never amiss,
And that now marvels me.
His father can I not find, iwis,
For all my craft, nor my quaintyce;   *cunning*
It seems he thought heaven were his
So stout a sire is he.

Since the world first began
Knew I never such a man,
Born of a mortal woman,
Though she is blameless.
Among the sinful, sin doth he none,
And cleaner than ever was anyone,
He seems to be of blood and bone,
And wiser than ever man was.

Avarice nor no envy
In him would I never espy;
He hath no gold in treasury,
Nor tempted is he by no sight.
Pride has he none, nor gluttony,
Nor no liking of lechery;
His mouth heard I never lie,
Neither day nor night.

(*noticing* JESUS)

And this thing dare I soothly say;
If that he were God verray,   *true*
Hunger should grieve him by no way;
That were against reason.
Therefore now I will assay
With speech of bread him to betray,
For he has fasted many a day,
Now meat were in season.

(*He approaches* JESUS.)

Thou man, abide and speak with me.
God's son, if that thou be,
Make of these stones that thou may see
Bread through thy blessing.

JESUS: Satan, I tell thee, surely,
Man lives not by bread only,
But through God's word, verily,
Of His mouth coming.

SATAN: Out! Alas! What is this?
This matter fares all amiss;
For hungry I see that he is,
As man should naturally be.
Some other sleight I must employ
This dosey-beard for to destroy,
For of me he hath the mastery,
Unhappily I see.

But I will seek some subtlety.

(*He beckons to* JESUS.)

Come forth, thou, Jesus, come with me
Unto the holy city;
I have one thing to say.

(JESUS *goes with* SATAN *to a high place representing a
pinnacle of the Temple.*)

Very God if that thou be
Now I shall full soon see,

For I shall ordain honour for thee,
Before you wend away.   *go*

(*He runs down and calls up to* JESUS)

Say, thou that sits there so high,
If thou be God's son, be sly,
Jump down and I will say I see
A wondrous feat of trickery.
Thine own angels may keep thee,
That thou hurt neither foot nor knee;
Show thou power, now let's see,
Thou may have honour thereby.

JESUS: Satan, truly I thee say:
It is written thou never may
Tempt God thy Lord, by no way,
What matter so ever be moved.

(JESUS *descends*.)

SATAN: Alas! Woe is me today!
Twice have I failed with my prey,
Was I never routed in such a way,
Nor so foully reproved.

(SATAN *leads* JESUS *to another high place – a mountain-top*.)

But yet, if it be thy will,
Go we play us upon this hill,
Another point thou must fulfill
For ought that may befall.
Look about thee now and see
Of all these realms the royalty;
If you kneel down and honour me
Thou shalt be Lord of all!

JESUS: Go forth, Satan! Go forth, go!
It is written and shall be so,
God, thy Lord, thou shalt honour mo
And serve him, though it thee noye.   *harm*

SATAN: Out! Alas! Now me is woe,
For found I never so mickle a foe;

127

Though I dispute, I fear it is so.
I am overcome thrice!

(SATAN *exits and* JESUS *descends and faces the people.*)

JESUS: Blessed are the poor in spirit:
For theirs is the kingdom of heaven.
Blessed are they that mourn:
For they shall be comforted.
Blessed are the meek:
For they shall inherit the earth.
Blessed are they which do hunger and thirst after
    righteousness:
For they shall be filled.
Blessed are the merciful:
For they shall obtain mercy.
Blessed are the pure in heart:
For they shall see God.
Blessed are the peacemakers:
For they shall be called the children of God.
Blessed are they which are persecuted for
    righteousness' sake:
For theirs is the kingdom of heaven.
Blessed are ye, when men shall revile you, and
    persecute you,
And shall say all manner of evil against you falsely for
    my sake.
Rejoice and be exceeding glad:
For great is your reward in heaven:
For so persecuted they the prophets which were before
    you.

(*Exit* JESUS *and a* SCRIBE *and* ACCUSER *who have been
listening run to meet a* PHARISEE.)

SCRIBE: Alas, alas, our law is lorne!   *destroyed*
A false hypocrite, Jesus by name,
That of a shepherd's daughter was born
Will break our law and make it lame.

ACCUSER: On him believe many a score,
For his preaching holds such sway,
Each man him follow the more and more,

128

Against that he saith no man saith nay.

PHARISEE: A false quarrel if we could feign,
That hypocrite to put in blame,
All his teaching would all disclaim,
And then his worship would turn to shame!

ACCUSER: Hark, sir Pharisee, and sir Scribe!
A right good sport I can you tell,
I can devise a wondrous jibe,
If that you will keep counsel.
A fair young woman hereby doth dwell,
Both fresh and gay upon to look,
And a tall man with her doth mell,
The way unto her chamber right he took.

Let us three now go straight thither:
That way, be sure, I shall you lead,
And we shall take them both together
While that they do that sinful deed.

SCRIBE: Art thou certain that we shall speed?
Shall we him find when we come there?

ACCUSER: By my troth, I have no dread
We shall catch them as they pair!

PHARISEE: We shall have game, if this be true.
Let us three work by one assent:
We will bring her even before Jesu,
And of her life the truth present,
How in adultery her life is spent.
Then him before, when she is brought,
We shall him ask the true judgement,
What lawful death for her is wrought.

Of grace and mercy ever he doth preach,
And that no man should be vengeful.
So, if he will *do* as he will teach,
To her he must be merciful.
And if we find him variable
In his preaching that he has taught,
Then have we cause both just and able
For a false man that he be caught.

SCRIBE: *But* if he hold still his dalliance
  And preach mercy, her for to save,
  Then we have matter of great substance
  Him for to kill and put in grave.
  Great reason why I shall you tell:
  For Moses doth bid in our law
  That every adulterer we should quell,
  And with cruel stones they should be slaw.   *slain*

ACCUSER: Ye tarry over-long, sirs, I say you,
  They will soon part, as that I guess;
  Therefore, if ye will have your prey now,
  Let us go take them in their wantonness.

PHARISEE: Go thou before, our way to guide,
  We shall thee follow in short while;
  They may try their shame to hide
  But we shall soon Jesu beguile.

  (*They approach a doorway.*)

SCRIBE: Break up the door and go we in,
  Set to thy shoulder with all thy might.
  We shall take them even in their sin,
  Their own trespass shall them indict.

  (*They force open the door. A* YOUNG MAN *runs out in his doublet, his shoes in his hand, holding up his breeches.*)

ACCUSER: Arrest the harlot, and hold her tight
  That in adultery here is found!

YOUNG MAN: If any man stows me this night
  I shall give him a deadly wound!

  (*drawing a dagger*)

  If any man my way doth stop,
  Ere we depart, dead shall he be.
  I shall this dagger put in his crop,
  I shall him kill ere he shall me!

PHARISEE: Great God's curse now go with thee!
  With such a shrew I will not mell.   *be concerned with*

YOUNG MAN: That same blessing I give you three,

130

And bequeath you all to the devil of hell!

(*to audience*)

In faith, I was so sore afraid
Of yon three shrews, the sooth to say,
My breech be not yet well uptied,
I had such haste to run away.

(*Exit.*)

SCRIBE: Come forth, thou stot; come forth, thou   *cow;*
     scout!   *animal*
     Come forth, thou bismer and brothel bold!   *lewd creature*
     Come forth, thou whore and stinking bitchclout!
     How long hast thou such harlotry hold?

(*The* WOMAN *is dragged forward.*)

WOMAN: Ah, mercy, mercy, sirs, I you pray;
     For God's love have mercy on me!
     Of my misliving me not betray;
     Have mercy on me for charity!

ACCUSER: Ask us no mercy: it shall not be.
     We shall so ordain for thy lot
     That thou shalt die for thine adultery.
     Therefore come forth, thou stinking stot!

WOMAN: Sirs, my worship if ye will save,
     And help I have no open shame,
     Both gold and silver ye shall have,
     So that in cleanness ye keep my name.

PHARISEE: Though thou like it thee never so ill,
     Before the prophet thou shalt have law:
     Like as Moses doth charge us till,
     With great stones thou shalt be slaw.

(JESUS *enters; the* WOMAN *is taken to him.* JESUS *bends down and writes on the ground with his finger, ignoring the accusations.*)

PHARISEE: Hark, Sir Prophet! We all you pray
     To give true doom and just sentence
     Upon this woman, which this same day

131

In sinful adultery hath done offence.

ACCUSER: See, we have brought her to your presence
Because ye be a wise prophet,
That ye shall tell by conscience
What death for her ye think most meet.

SCRIBE: In Moses' law right thus we find:
That such false lovers shall be slain;
Straight to a stake we shall them bind,
And with great stones burst out their brain.
Of your conscience tell us it plain,
With this woman what shall be wrought:
Shall we let her go quit again,
Or to her death shall she be brought?

(JESUS *still does not reply, but goes on writing with his finger.*)

WOMAN: Now, Holy Prophet, be merciable!
Upon me, wretch, take no vengeance.
For my sins abominable,
In heart I have great repentance.

ACCUSER: Have done, Sir Prophet, tell us your lore:
Shall we this woman with stones kill
Or to her house and home restore?
In this matter tell us your will.

SCRIBE: In a cold study methinks you sit,
Good sir, awake, tell us your thought.
Shall she be stoned? Tell us your wit,
Or by what rule shall she be brought?

(JESUS *stands and looks at them.*)

JESUS: Look which of you that never sin wrought,
But is of life cleaner than she,
Cast the first stone, and spare her nought.
Clean out of sin if that ye be.

(*He squats down and writes again. The* WOMAN *has sunk to the ground in grief. The* ACCUSERS, *put to shame, slink away.*)

JESUS: (*looking up at the* WOMAN)

> Where be thy foemen that did thee accuse?
> Why have they left us two alone?

WOMAN: Because they could not themselves excuse,
> With shame have they fled, every one.

JESUS: For those sins that thou hast wrought
> Hath any man condemned thee?

WOMAN: Nay, forsooth, that hath there nought;
> But in your grace I put me.

JESUS: For me, thou shalt not condemned be,
> Go home again and walk at large:
> Look that thou live in honesty,
> And sin no more, I now thee charge.

(*The* WOMAN *pauses, then runs off.*)

> What man of sin be repentant,   *whatever*
> Of God if he will mercy crave,
> God of mercy is so abundant,
> That what man ask, he shall have!

THE MINISTRY: HEALING, TEACHING AND PLOTTING

CHARACTERS

JESUS

MARTHA

MARY

LAZARUS

TWO BEGGARS

MARY MAGDALENE

JUDAS

JOHN

ANNAS

FOUR DOCTORS

ARFEX

CAIAPHAS

RUFFIN

LEON

THE MINISTRY: HEALING,
TEACHING AND PLOTTING

(JESUS *enters with his disciples*.)

JESUS: Come now, brethren, and go with me,
We will pass forth unto Judea;
To Bethany will we wend,
To visit Lazarus, who is our friend.
Gladly I would we with him speak,
I tell you surely, he is sick.

(*Enter* MARTHA *who falls at* JESUS' *feet*.)

MARTHA: Help me, Lord, in my most need!
Lazarus, my brother, now is dead,
That was to thee both loved and dear;
He had not died had thou been here.

JESUS: Martha, Martha, from grief refrain,
Thy brother shall rise and live again.

MARTHA: Lord, I know full well that he *shall* rise
And stand before the great justice;
For at the dreadful day of doom
Then shall he come forth from the tomb,
To find what doom thou wilt him give,
Then must he rise, *then* will he live.

JESUS: I tell you all, both man and wife,
I am the resurrection and the life,
And who so truly believes in me,
That I was ever and aye shall be,
One thing I shall him give,
Though he be dead, yet shall he live.
Say thou, woman, believest thou this?

MARTHA: Yea, forsooth, my Lord of bliss,
Thou comest to me in this my need,
For all your words are truth indeed.

JESUS: Go tell thy sister Mary

That her Lord is coming again.

(MARTHA *runs to* MARY *who is with a band of mourners*.)

MARTHA: Sister, leave this sorrowful band,
Our Lord comes here at hand
And his apostles with him also.

MARY: Ah, for God's love let me go.
Blessed be he that sends me grace,
That I may see Him in this place.

(*Goes to* JESUS.)

Lord, much sorrow may men see
Of my sister here and me;
We are heavy as any lead,
For our brother that thus is dead.
Had thou been here and had him seen,
Dead forsooth had he not been.

JESUS: Hither we are come to you
To bring you comfort in your care.
But look that faint heart nor no sloth
Takes you from the steadfast truth;
Then I shall do e'en as I said.
Lo, where have ye his body laid?

MARY: Lord, if it be thy will,
I think by now he savers ill,   *smells*
For it is now the third day gone
Since he was laid under yonder stone.

JESUS: I told thee right now where thou stood
That thy truth should aye be good!

(*He kneels to pray outside the tomb*.)

Father, I pray thee that thou raise
Lazarus, that servant of thine,
And bring him out of his suffering
In hell no more to pine.   *suffer*
When I pray, thou sayest in all ways
My will is such as thine.
Therefore we will prolong his days,

138

To me thou wilt incline.

Come forth, Lazarus, and stand us by;
In earth shall thou no longer lie!

(LAZARUS *comes from the tomb, the grave-clothes still
wrapped round him; there is astonishment.*)

Take and loose him foot and hand
And from his throat take the band,
And the shroud take him fro,
And all that gear, and let him go.   *wrapping*

(*Some onlookers approach* LAZARUS *and do as* JESUS *says.*)

LAZARUS: (*approaching* JESUS *after embracing his sisters*)

Lord, that all things made of nought,
Loving be to thee,
That such wonder here has wrought,
Greater may none be.
When I was dead to hell I sought
And thou through thy power
Raised me up, and thence me brought.
Behold and ye may see!

MARTHA: (*Addressing the audience and by-standers*)

He is a Lord of grace.
Meditate on this case,
And pray him, full of might,
He keep you in this place
And have you in his sight.

(*Enter two blind* BEGGARS.)

FIRST BEGGAR: Thou son of David, on us have mercy!
As we must steadfastly believe in thee,
Thy goodness, Lord, let us be nigh,
Who lieth blind here and may not see.

SECOND BEGGAR: Lord, let thy mercy to us be shown
And restore to us our bodily health.
The smallest morsel from thy throne
Brings to our longing hearts great wealth.

JESUS: Your faith hath made you for to see
And delivered you from all mortal pain.
Blessed be all that believe in me,
And see me not with earthly eyne.

(*He reaches out his hand slowly and touches their eyes.*)

FIRST BEGGAR: Gramercy, Lord, of thy great grace:
I that was blind now may see!

SECOND BEGGAR: Here I forsake all my trespass
And steadfastly will believe in thee.

(*Sick people are brought to* JESUS *and in silence he heals them.*)

MARY MAGDALENE: As a cursed creature, clothed all in
care,
And as a wicked wretch, all wrapped in woe,
Of bliss was never a woman so bare
As I myself that here now go.
Alas, alas! I might despair,
But, though many great sins I do,
They are less than my great Lord's care,
And his great mercy can receive me to.
Mary Magdalene is my name,
Now will I go to Christ Jesu
For he is Lord of all virtue,
To rid me of my shame.

(MARY *goes to* JESUS *who has sat on a stool with his disciples around him; they are drinking.*)

Ah, mercy, Lord, and cleanse my sins!
Maiden's flower, thou wash me free!
There was never woman of man's kin
So full of sin in no country.

(*Kneeling at* JESUS' *feet*)

MARY MAGDALENE: I have transgressed in wood and fen,
And sought sin in many a city,
Unless thou me save, Lord, I shall burn,
With black fiends ever doomed to be.

140

(**MARY** *anoints* **JESUS'** *feet with ointment and dries them with her long hair*.)

Wherefore, king of grace,
With this ointment that is so sweet,
Let me anoint thy holy feet,
And from my wickedness win some release.
Mercy, Lord, for my trespass!

JESUS: (*lifting her gently by the hand*)

Woman, for thy weeping, will
Some succour God thee send.
Thee to save I have great skill.
For a sorrowful heart may sin amend.
All thy prayers I shall fulfill;
To thy good heart I will attend,
And save thee from thy sin so vile
And from the devil thee defend.

(*Sternly, as if casting out spirits*)

Fiends, flee away!
Wicked spirits, I you conjure,
Leave at once her bodily bower!
In my grace she shall ever flower
Till death bear her away.

JUDAS: (*with irony*)

Lord, me thinketh thou dost right well
To let this ointment so spill.
To sell it were more skill,
And buy meat for poor men.
The box was worth in good money
Three hundred pence, fair and free.
This might have bought meat in plenty
To feed our poor kindred.

JESUS: Judas, the poor are always with us;
Against this woman thou speakest wrong.
And, from this moment on,
Of mercy shall be her morning song!

Friends, behold the time of mercy,

The which is come now without doubt.
Man's soul in bliss now shall edify,
And the prince of this world is cast out.
Go to yon castle that standeth you again,
Some of my disciples, go forth ye two;
There shall ye find beasts twain –
An ass tied and her foal also.
Unloose that ass and bring it to me plain.
If any ask why that ye so do,
Say that I have need of this beast, certain,
And he shall not stand in your way;
That beast bring ye to me.

JOHN: Holy prophet, we go our way.
We will not at your word delay,
And, as soon as that we may,
We shall it bring to thee.

(*Exeunt all.*)

(*enter* ANNAS *and* DOCTORS, *all richly attired.*)

ANNAS: As I am prelate, I am empowered to provide peace,
And, as judge of the Jews, the law to fortify.
I, Annas, by my powers shall command, doubtless,
The laws of Moses no man shall deny.
Now, Sirs, for a story hear mine intent.
There is one Jesus of Nazareth that our laws doth exceed.
If he proceed thus we shall us all repent,
For our laws he destroyeth daily with his deed.

Therefore by your counsel we must take heed
What is best to provide or do in this case.
For if we let him thus go and further proceed,
Against Caesar and our law we do trespass.

FIRST DOCTOR: Sir, this is my advice that ye shall do:
Send to Caiaphas for counsel, know his intent.
For if Jesus proceed and thus forth go,
Our laws shall be destroyed, this I thee present.

SECOND DOCTOR: Sir, remember the great charge that on
    you is laid,
The law to keep, which may not fail.
If any proven fault of yours be said,
The Jews, in truth, will you assail.
Take heed what counsel may prevail:
For Ruffin and Leon I suggest you send,
They are temporal judges, who know the way
With your cousin Caiaphas this matter to amend.

ANNAS: Now surely this counsel revives my heart.
Your advice is best as I can see.
Arfex, in haste look that thou start
And pray Caiaphas, my cousin, come speak with me.

To Ruffin and Leon go thou also,
And pray them to speak with me in haste
On a vital matter that we must do,
And must be done ere this day be passed.

ARFEX: My sovereign, at your intent I shall be gone
In all the haste that I can hie
Unto Caiaphas, Ruffin and Leon,
And charge their intent that they shall ply.

(ARFEX *goes to* CAIAPHAS, *who appears, gaudily dressed,
with his entourage of learned doctors.*)

CAIAPHAS: As a primate most prudent, I present here,
    visible,
Bishops of the law with all circumstance.
I, Caiaphas, am judge, with powers possible
To destroy all errors that to our laws make variance.
But there is one, Christ, that our laws makes variable,
He perverts the people with his preaching ill.
We must seek a means, with my cousin Annas,
To destroy him, or our law he will spill.

THIRD DOCTOR: My Lord, please you to pardon what I say,
The blame in you is as we find,
To let Christ continue thus day by day
With false witchcraft the people to blind.

FOURTH DOCTOR: Forsooth, Sir, of truth this is the case;

On to our law you put oppression,
That ye let Christ go from place to place
And will not put on him correction.

CAIAPHAS: Well, Sirs, ye shall see within a short while
I shall correct him out of his trespass:
He shall no longer our people beguile;
Out of my danger he shall not pass.

(*Enter* ARFEX, RUFFIN *and* LEON. ARFEX *kneels before*
CAIAPHAS.)

ARFEX: My reverent sovereign, and it do you please,
Sir Annas, my Lord, hath to you sent.
He prays that you will not cease
Till that ye be with him present.

CAIAPHAS: Sir, tell my cousin I shall not fail,
It was my purpose him for to see,
For certain matters that will prevail
Though he had not sent for me.

ARFEX: (*To* RUFFIN *and* LEON)

Hail, Judges of Jewry, of reason most prudent:
Of my message to you I make relation.
My Lord, Sir Annas, hath for you sent
To see his presence without delacion.   *delay*

RUFFIN: Sir, we are ready at his commandment
To see Sir Annas in his place.
It was our purpose and our intent
To be with him within short space.

(LEON, RUFFIN *and* CAIAPHAS *meet and whisper together*
while ARFEX *returns to* ANNAS.)

CAIAPHAS: Now on to Annas let us wend
Each of us to know the other's intent.
Many matters I have in mind
The which to him I shall present.

(CAIAPHAS *and all the* DOCTORS *with* RUFFIN *and* LEON *go to*
ANNAS.)

ANNAS: Welcome, Sir Caiaphas, and ye judges all!

Now shall ye know all mine intent.
A wondrous case, Sirs, here is befall
On which we must give judgement.
Lest that we after the case repent,
This Christ, that God's son doth him call,
He showeth miracles, and himself presents
That he is prince of princes all!

CAIAPHAS: He saith in every place
That he is King of Jews in every degree,
Therefore he is false, know well the case;
Caesar is king and none but he.

RUFFIN: He is a heretic and a traitor bold
To Caesar and to our law most certain,
Both in word and in work and ye behold;
He is worthy to die with much pain.

LEON: The cause that we here present
To fortify the law and truth to say.
Jesus, full near our law hath shent,   *disgraced*
Therefore, he is worthy to die.

FIRST DOCTOR: Sirs, ye that be rulers of the law,
On Jesus ye must give judgement.
Let him first be hanged and draw,
And then his body in fire burnt.

SECOND DOCTOR: Now shall you hear intent of me:
Take Jesus that bringeth us all great shame,
Put him to death – let him not flee –
For else the commoners will you blame.

ANNAS: Now, brethren, then will he hear my intent.
These nine days let us abide,
We must not give so hasty judgement,
But each man enquire on his side,
Send spies about the country wide
To see and record and testify:
And then his words he shall not hide
Nor have no power them to deny.

CAIAPHAS: This counsel accordeth to my reason.

ANNAS: Then we are all agreed!

145

THE ENTRY INTO JERUSALEM

2

CHARACTERS

PETER
JOHN
FOUR CITIZENS

THE ENTRY INTO JERUSALEM

(A crowd has gathered. PETER *and* JOHN *enter.)*

PETER: O, ye people despairing, be glad!
A great cause ye have as you shall see;
The Lord that all things of naught has made
Is coming, your comfort for to be.
All your sicknesses heal shall he;
He comes to satisfy the meek,
He shall cause the blind that they shall see,
The deaf to hear, the dumb for to speak.

JOHN: Now, brothers in God, since we have intelligence
That our Lord is nye come to this city,
To attend upon his precious presence,
It falls to us, as it seems to me,
To meet him most reverently –
I would for nothing that we were too late.
To the city-ward fast draweth he,
Me thinketh he is bye at the gate.

1ST CITIZEN: Neighbours, great joy in our hearts we may
make
That this heavenly king will visit this city.

2ND CITIZEN: If our earthly king such a journey should
take
To do him honour and worship busy should we be.

3RD CITIZEN: Much more than to the heavenly king bound
are we
For to do that should be to his person, reverence.

4TH CITIZEN: Let us then welcome him with flowers and
branches of the tree
Because, in the sweet perfume, great pleasure will there
be.

*(The citizens take branches and flowers and spread their
clothes in the path of* JESUS, *some kneeling. They wave their
branches calling 'Hosanna! Hosanna!')*

149

1ST CITIZEN: Now, blessed be he that cometh in the name
of the Lord!

2ND CITIZEN: Hosanna to the son of David!

3RD CITIZEN: Thou son of David, be thou our support
At our last day when we shall die!

(JESUS *dismounts and continues up the steps on foot.*)

THE LAST SUPPER

3

CHARACTERS

JESUS
PETER
JOHN
SIMON
JUDAS

THE LAST SUPPER

(JESUS *looks over Jerusalem and weeps: He speaks to his disciples.*)

JESUS: O Jerusalem, woeful is the ordinance
   Of the day of thy great persecution!
   Thou shalt be destroyed with woeful grievance
   And be brought low with true confusion.
   They that in the city have habitation,
   They shall curse the time that they were born,
   So great adversity and tribulation
   Shall fall on them both evening and morn.

   They that have most children soonest shall wail,
   And say 'Alas! What may this mean?'
   Both meat and drink suddenly shall fail,
   The vengeance of God there shall be seen.
   The time is coming, his woe shall descend,
   The day of trouble and great grievance,
   Both temple and towers, they shall fall down clean
   O city, full woeful is this ordinance!

PETER: (*unsure how to approach* JESUS, *who is still weeping,*)

   Lord, where wilt thou keep thy Passover?
   I pray thee now let us have knowing,
   That we may make ready for thee,
   Thee to serve without hindrance.

JOHN: To provide, Lord, for thy coming
   With all the obedience we can attend,
   And make ready for thee in all thing
   Into what place thou wilt us send.

JESUS: Sirs, go to Zion and ye shall meet
   A poor man in simple array
   Bearing water in the street.
   Tell him I shall come that way.

PETER: At thy will Lord, it shall be done:
   To seek that place we shall us hie.

go

JOHN: In all haste that we may go
Thy commandment never to deny.

(JESUS *withdraws.* PETER *and* JOHN *go onward and meet*
SIMON THE LEPER *carrying a pitcher of water.*)

PETER: Good man, the prophet our Lord Jesus
This night will rest within thine hall.
With this message to thee hath he sent us,
That for his supper prepare thou shall.

SIMON: What, will my Lord visit my place?
Blessed be the time of his coming!
I shall ordain within short space
For my good Lord's welcoming.

(*He takes them with him and they are joined by the other
disciples, who assist in setting up a trestle table, benches and
a simple meal of meat, bread and wine. When it is ready,*
JESUS *enters.*)

PETER: All ready, Lord, is our feast,
As I hope to you pleasing shall be.

SIMON: Gracious Lord, welcome thou be,
Reverence be to thee both God and man.
My poor house I give willingly,
To show I am thy servant as I can.

(JESUS *lays a hand on his arm and then signals them to sit
round the table.* JUDAS *keeps a little apart,* JOHN *sits very
close to* JESUS. *They begin to eat.*)

JESUS: Brethren, this lamb that is set us before,
That we all have eaten this night,
It was commanded by my father to Moses in law
When they were with the children of Israel in Egypt.
With a fervent desire of my heart's affection,
I have entirely desired to keep my Maund
Among you, before I suffer my passion.
For of this, no more together sup shall we
And, as the paschal lamb eaten have we
In the old law was used for a sacrifice,
So the new lamb, that shall be sacred by me,

Shall be used for a sacrifice most of price.

(JESUS *takes bread and looks to Heaven, saying*)

Wherefore, to the Father in heaven that art eternal,
Thanks and honour I yield, that Thou wilt show this
    mystery,
And thus through Thy might, Father, and blessing of
    me,
Of this that was bread is made my body.

(*He breaks the bread and distributes it to all except* JUDAS.)

This is my body, flesh and blood
That for Thee shall die upon the rood.

(*As He comes to give bread to* JUDAS)

Judas, art thou aware what thou shalt take?

JUDAS: Lord, thy body I will not forsake.

JESUS: My body to thee I will not deny
    Since thou wilt presume thereupon.

(*He sits.*)

One of you hath betrayed me,
That at my board with me hath ate,
Better for him to have been
Both unborn and unbeget.

(*Each disciple looks at the others until* PETER *speaks.*)

PETER: Lord, is it I?

(*Each disciple except* JUDAS *says this.*)

JUDAS: Is it ought I, Lord?

JESUS: Judas, thou sayest that word.
    Me thou hast sold that was thy friend.
    That thou must do, bring to an end.

(JUDAS *leaves; they all watch him go.*)

Now the son of God glorified is,
And God in him is glorified also
But now in memory of my passion,

For to dwell with me in my kingdom above,
Ye shall drink my blood with great devotion,
Which shall be shed for man's love.

(*He takes the cup, blesses it and passes it amongst them.*)

Take this chalice of the New Testament,
And keep this ever in your mind.
As often as ye do this with true intent,
It shall defend you from the fiend.

This is my blood that, for man's sin,
Out of my heart shall run.

Whoso eateth my body and drinketh my blood,
Whole God and man he shall partake!

(JESUS *takes a basin of water and wraps a towel around his waist. He kneels in front of* PETER.)

Another example I shall you show,
How ye shall live in charity,
Sit here down with words few
And what I do ye must suffer me.

(*He goes to wash* PETER's *feet.*)

PETER: Lord, what wilt thou with me do?
This service of thee I will forsake;
To wash my feet thou shalt not so:
I am not worthy it of thee to take.

JESUS: Peter, if thou forsake my service all,
The which to you I shall do,
No part with me have thou shall
And never come my bliss unto.

PETER: That part, Lord, we will not forgo.
We shall obey his commandment,
Wash head and hand we pray thee so,
We will follow thine intent.

(JESUS *washes the disciples' feet, drying them with the towel. Then He again sits at the table.*)

JESUS: Friends, this washing shall now prevail,

Your lord and master ye do me call,
And so I am without fail,
Yet I have washed you all;
A memory of this have you all
That each of you shall do to the other;
With humble heart, submit equal,
As each of you were the other's brother.

Now, this night from you be led I shall,
And ye for fear from me shall flee,
Not one durst speak when I you call
And some of you forsake me.
For you shall I die and rise again;
On the third day ye shall me see
Before you, all walking plain
In the land of Galilee.

PETER: Lord, I will never thee forsake,
Nor for no perils from thee flee,
I will rather my death take
Than once, Lord, forsake thee.

JESUS: Peter – in further than thou dost know –
As for that, promises look thou not make,
For before the cock hath twice crow,
Thrice thou shall me forsake.

(*He silently prevents* PETER'S *protests.*)

But, all my friends that are to me dear,
Let us go, the time draweth near,
We may no longer abide here,
For I must walk to Bethany.

The time is come; the day draweth near;
On to my death I must haste.
Now, Peter, give all thy fellows cheer,
My flesh for fear is quaking fast.

(*They stand and leave.*)

THE BETRAYAL

6

CHARACTERS

JUDAS
GAMALIEL
RUFFIN
LEON
JESUS
PETER
ANGEL
MARY

THE BETRAYAL

(RUFFIN, LEON, GAMALIEL *and other Jews as if in conference together. Enter* JUDAS *running.*)

JUDAS: Hail, princes and priests that be present!
New tidings to you I come to tell,
If ye will follow mine intent,
My master Jesu I will you sell.

GAMALIEL: Now welcome, Judas, our own friend.
Take him in, Sirs, by the hand.
We shall thee both give and lend,
And in every quarrel by thee stand.

RUFFIN: Judas, what shall we for thy master pay?
The silver is ready; and, if we accord,
The payment shall have no delay
But be laid down here at a word.

JUDAS: Let the money here down be laid,
And I shall tell you as I can.
In old times I heard it was said
That money maketh a merchant man.

RUFFIN: Here are thirty pieces of silver bright
Fast tied within this glove,
If we may have thy master this night,
Then thou shalt have all our love.

LEON: There be many that him never saw
Which we will send to him in fear;
Therefore by a token we must him know,
That must be privy betwixt us here.

JUDAS: As for that, Sirs, have ye no doubt,
I shall ordain so ye shall not miss,
When that ye come him about,
Take the man that I shall kiss.

(*They toss* JUDAS *the money and go out laughing, leaving him to pick up the coins. Exit* JUDAS. JESUS *enters with his disciples.*)

161

JESUS: Now, my dear friends and brethren each one,
     Remember the words that I shall say;
     The time is come that I must be gone
     For to fulfill the prophecy.

(*They reach the Garden of Gethsemane.*)

     Peter, with thy fellows here shalt thou abide,
     And watch till I come again,
     I must make my prayer here you beside;
     My flesh quaketh sore for fear and pain.

PETER: Lord, thy request doth me constrain
     In this place I shall abide still.

(JESUS *goes a short distance away, falls to his knees and prays.*)

JESUS: O Father, Father, for my sake
     This awful cup thou take from me,
     Which is ordained that I should take
     If man's soul saved should be.

(JESUS *rises and goes to* PETER *and the other disciples, and finds them sleeping.*)

     Peter, Peter, thou sleepest fast;
     Awake thy fellows and sleep no more!
     Of my death are ye not aghast?
     Ye take your rest and I suffer sore!

(JESUS *goes and prays again.*)

     Father in heaven, I beseech thee,
     Remove my pains by thy great grace,
     And let me from this torment flee,
     As I did never trespass.
     The drops of sweat upon my face
     Distil for pains that I shall take.
     My flesh quaketh in fearful case
     As though the joints assunder would shake.

(JESUS *goes to his* DISCIPLES *again and finds them sleeping. He lets them sleep and prays again.*)

     Father, the third time I come again

To plead my cause before thy face
Deliver me, Father, from this pain,
Sustain my spirit through thy grace.
Unto thy son, Father, take heed.
Thou knowest I have done nought but good,
It is not for me that I must bleed
But for man I sweat both water and blood.

(*An* ANGEL *appears and holds out a chalice to* JESUS.)

ANGEL: Hail, both God and man indeed!
The Father hath sent thee this present
He bad that thou should'st not dread
But fulfill his intent.
This chalice is thy blood,
For man's sin ever offered shall be
To thy Father of heaven that is almighty,
Thy disciples and all priesthood shall offer for thee.

(*The* ANGEL *departs.*)

JESUS: Father, thy will fulfilled shall be.

(*A noisy crowd is heard approaching: they enter, carrying swords, sticks and torches.*)

Rise up, sirs, I you pray.

(*The disciples stand confused and* JESUS *goes to confront the crowd which is led by* JUDAS.)

Sirs, in your way ye have great haste
To seek him that will not flee,
Tell me, Sirs, whom seek ye?

LEON: Whom we seek here I tell thee now:
A traitor who is worthy to suffer death.
We know he is here among you.
His name is Jesus of Nazareth.

(*The crowd presses forward.*)

JESUS: Sirs, I am here and will not flee,
Do to me all that ye can.
For sooth to tell you, I am he,
Jesus of Nazareth, that same man.

(The crowd falls back.)

I say again, whom seek ye?

RUFFIN: Jesus of Nazareth we seek,
If we might him here espy.

JESUS: I told you now with words meek
Before you all that it was I.

JUDAS: Welcome, Jesu, my master dear,
I have thee sought in many a place.
I am full glad to find thee here
For I wist never where thou wast.   *knew*

(JUDAS goes to JESUS and kisses him. The mob takes hold of JESUS.)

PETER: I draw my sword now this time.
Shall I smite, master? Fain would I know.

(He slashes off the ear of MALCHUS, a servant, who cries 'My ear, my ear!' JESUS heals the wound.)

JESUS: Put up thy sword, Peter,
He that liveth by the sword shall die by the sword!

LEON: Bring forth this traitor! Spare him nought!
Unto Caiaphas, thy judge, we shall thee lead.
In many places we have thee sought,
And to thy works have taken good heed.

RUFFIN: Come on, Jesus, and follow me.
I am full glad that I thee have,
Thou shalt be hanged upon a tree;
A million of gold shall not thee save!

(JESUS is led away. Enter the VIRGIN MARY, who watches the party leave.)

MARY: Ah, Jesu! Jesu! Jesu! Jesu!
Why should ye suffer this tribulation and adversity?
How may they find in their hearts you to pursue
That never trespassed in no manner of degree?
For never a thing but that was good thought ye.
Wherefore then should he suffer this great pain?

I suppose, verily, it is for the trespass of me;
And I wist that my heart would cleave in twain.   *know*

Now dear son, since thou hast ever been so full of
    mercy,
Think on thy mother, that heavy woman!

THE TRIAL OF JESUS

CHARACTERS

JESUS

THREE TORTURERS

CAIAPHAS

ANNAS

A WOMAN

A SERVANT GIRL

PETER

A JEW

PILATE

A CROWD

HEROD

THE TRIAL OF JESUS

(*Enter* JESUS *driven by two torturers*.)

1ST TORTURER: Get on there, go! Trot on apace,
To Annas will we go and Sir Caiaphas;
Be sure, of them two thou gettest no grace,
But everlasting woe for the trespass thou has
So great.
Thy fate is to fare
Far worse there
Than thou hast been anywhere,
False traitor to the state!

(*Enter* ANNAS *and* CAIAPHAS.)

2ND TORTURER: Hail, sirs, full of power and might,
Why ask you not how we have fared this night?

CAIAPHAS: Can you him impeach? Fled his friends in fear?

1ST TORTURER: Aye, and he has been heard to preach for
many a year.

2ND TORTURER: Sir, I heard him say he would destroy our
temple so gay
And then build it anew on the third day.

CAIAPHAS: How might that be true? It took much to
array,   *build*
The masons I knew that hewed it I say,
So wise, that hewed every stone.

1ST TORTURER: Ah, good sir, let him alone,
He lies – for a smooth tongue
I give him the prize.

CAIAPHAS: Now attend and cease your talking,
For now I myself will begin examining.

(*To* JESUS.)

Harlot of all; with care may you sing!
Harken,

How darst thou thee call emperor or king?
I defy thee!
What the devil dost thou here?
Thy deeds will cost thee dear.
Come now, and whisper in mine ear,
Or I shall decry thee.

(JESUS *does not speak.*)

Speak but one word now in the devil's name!

(JESUS *is still silent.*)

Lad, I am a prelate, a lord in degree,
All in my estate as thou may'st see.

ANNAS: (*To* CAIAPHAS)

Ah, sir, be not downcast, though he not answer;
He is inwardly routed, we must be gentler.

CAIAPHAS: A foul fate him befall!

ANNAS: Sir, be not so vexed withall,
And peradventure he shall
Hereafter please you.
We must by our law examine him first.

CAIAPHAS: Unless I give him a blow, my heart will burst!
I shall ring his neck that it may crack.

ANNAS: Some skill in this matter you do lack.

(*To* JESUS.)

Hark fellow, come here!

(JESUS *stays still.*)

Will you never beware?
I marvel you dare.
Say, did you this ill, canst thou excuse thee?
Why standst thou so still when men accuse thee?
Say, art thou God's son of heaven
As thou art wont for to claim?

JESUS: So thou sayest by the words,
And right so I am.

For after this shalt thou see me when that I come down
In brightness and in clouds from above.

CAIAPHAS: (*Rending his own garments*)

Ah, cursed be the feet that brought thee to town!
Thou art worthy to die I say, thief; where is thy crown?

1ST TORTURER: (*Taking* JESUS *and handing him a stool*)

Come sir, sit down. Must you be prayed?
Like a Lord of renown your seat is arrayed.

(JESUS *is forced to sit on the stool.*)

3RD TORTURER: Here is a veil – I hope it will last.

2ND TORTURER: Bring it hither good son, that's what I ask.

3RD TORTURER: How should it be done?

1ST TORTURER: About his head cast and, when you have
   well bound,
Tie the knot fast.

(JESUS *is blindfolded.*)

Now, since he is blindfold, I will begin,
He shall prophesy who smote his chin!

(*They strike him, jeering 'Prophesy, who smote thee?'* JESUS
does not reply and is eventually hauled up before CAIAPHAS
again.)

CAIAPHAS: Now, since he is well beaten, take him through
   the gate
And tell ye the charge unto Sir Pilate,
For he sits in the judgement chair among men of state,
And look that ye be not late!

1ST TORTURER: (*To* JESUS)

Come on old crate,
Believe me, we shall lead thee a trot.

(JESUS *is led away. Enter* PILATE *and a crowd – amongst
them is* PETER *who is unobtrusively trying to see what is
happening. He is spotted by a* WOMAN.)

171

WOMAN: Sir, do you not know this man?

PETER: Nay, I know him not, by him that made me!
If ye will believe me when I say as I do
I will swear before this company
That what I say is true!

SERVANT GIRL: Ah, good man, it seems to me
That one of his disciples you must be.

PETER: No, woman, I have never seen this man
Ever since the world began!

A JEW: Ah, fellow, welcome here!
You're the one who cropped my cousin's ear.
And now you may not flee away
For you are from Galilee, I dare say.

(*At this moment,* JESUS *is dragged through the crowd.*)

PETER: Man, thou sayest amiss of me!
I know him not, as I know not thee!

(*The cock crows twice.* JESUS *turns and looks at* PETER. PETER *weeps and runs out. Enter* CAIAPHAS *and* ANNAS. *They go to* PILATE *as* JESUS *is led to stand before him.* PILATE *is flanked by* SOLDIERS.)

CAIAPHAS: Sir Pilate, harken to this case.
Before thee, Jesus we have brought,
Who to our Law brings much disgrace,
And great distress hath wrought.

ANNAS: Yes, sir, more – nay worst of all –
Defying Caesar, our Emperor renowned,
The King of the Jews himself he calls,
And brings our Emperor's power down.

PILATE: Jesus, I understand thou art a King
And the Son of God; thou art also
Lord of Earth and of all thing:
Tell me if this be so.

JESUS: In Heaven is known my Father's intent:
But in this world I was born;
By my Father was I hither sent,

To comfort those that are forlorn.

PILATE: Now, sirs, you have heard this man.
How think you?
Think you not, using your reason,
That what he say may well be true?
I find in him no guilt or treason.

CAIAPHAS: The Emperor shall be told of this,
If you let Jesus thus depart.

PILATE: Then, tell me, sirs, one thing.
What shall be his charge?

ANNAS: Sir, we tell thee all together,
For his evil works we brought him hither.

PILATE: Take him then to your own court,
And judge him according to your law.

CAIAPHAS: For us, it is not lawful
To execute a criminal:
That is why we bring him thus,
For he shall not be King over us!

THE CROWD: Caesar is our king! Long live Caesar!

(PILATE *quietens the* MOB *and turns to* JESUS *again.*)

PILATE: Jesus, thou art King of the Jews?

JESUS: So thou sayest.

PILATE: Tell me then, where is thy kingdom?

JESUS: My kingdom is not of this world,
I tell thee in a word.
If my kingdom had been here
I never had been delivered to thee.

PILATE: Sirs, find some other judge if you can, I find no
error in this man.

(THE CROWD *shouts 'Condemn him to die!' etc.*)

Now, one thing make plain to me,
Was Jesus born in Galilee?

173

ANNAS: Sir, he was born in Bethlehem of Judea,
As all will tell who are assembled here,
And that stands in Galilee.

PILATE: Well, Sirs, the judgement of Jesus lies not with me,
For Herod is King of that country.
Therefore, commend me to Herod in word and deed,
And take Jesus before him with all speed.

(*Exit* PILATE. *Enter* HEROD. JESUS *is led before him.*)

HEROD: Now, by Mahomet, my god of grace,
This deed of Pilate's is truly kind;
I forgive him his great trespass
And will hereafter be his friend.
Jesus, thou are welcome to me.
I have desired so long thee to see,
To understand what your miracles be,
For I have heard great wonders of thee.
Now, Jesus, let me see,
A miracle wrought here, just for me!

(JESUS *remains impassive.*)

In haste now with all diligence,
Thou art in my presence!

(JESUS *is unmoved;* HEROD *rages.*)

Jesus, why speakest thou not to thy King?
What is the cause of thy squatting so still?
Thou knowest I am judge of all thing,
Thy life and death are in my will.
What! Speak, Jesus and tell me why
These people do you accuse.
Spare not – tell me openly
What is your excuse?

(JESUS *is still silent.*)

CAIAPHAS: Sire, this is his clever subtlety.
He speaketh not but when he chooses.

HEROD: What! Speak, I say! You foul slave,
Damn you with curses!

Look up! The devil will teach you.
Sirs, beat his body with scourges,
And make him speak!

(*They pull off* JESUS' *robe and flog him with whips and put a crown of thorns on his head.*)

1ST TORTURER: Jesus, thy bones may not break,
But we shall make thee skip.

2ND TORTURER: Thou mayest have lost thy tongue,
But you shall taste this whip.

(*They beat him until he is bloody;* HEROD *stops them in alarm.*)

HEROD: Cease, I command you by the devil of hell!
His errors never will he tell.
Sirs, take Jesus without further pain
And lead him back to Pilate again.
Greet him well and tell him straight
I give him power over Jesus.
Take him out of my sight!

(JESUS *is led away. Exit* HEROD. *Re-enter* PILATE.)

CAIAPHAS: Lord Pilate, Herod hath once more sent
Jesus to you, that you may give judgement.

PILATE: In Jesus I find no fault, not one,
Nor doth Herod, since he sends him on;
Therefore it is meet we let him be gone
Whither he will away.

JEW: Nail him, we cry with one voice!

CROWD: Nail him to the cross! Nail him!

PILATE: You men, for shame! Silence your din!
My counsel I will say.
You know the custom, each man here,
That I release to you a prisoner
On the Feastday that draws near.
Shall it be Jesus?

JEW: No! He is worthy to suffer death,

And so we cry with one breath,
Barrabas be reprieved!

CROWD: Barrabas! Barrabas!

PILATE: Ye prelates now, thinkest thou so!
What would ye do? Will you let him go?

CAIAPHAS: Nail him to the cross!

ANNAS: Condemn him!

PILATE: Jesus, tell me, I pray you, say
If you be king, say yes or no:
Are you King of the Jews?

JESUS: Do you hope that this should be
Or have men told you this of me?

PILATE: By the gods, you know and see
That I am no Jew.
Men of your own nation
Call for your damnation,
And have done so all this day.
Are you King, as some men say?

JESUS: I have told thee that my realm
Is not of this world, for if it were
No Jew would take me here.

PILATE: Therefore you are a king, or were?

JESUS: It is no more than you suggest;
But now I tell you, I confess
That King I am, and shall be King;
To the world I came to bear witness
To truth, and therefore was I born.

PILATE: Tell me Jesus, what is truth?

JESUS: It cometh from God's own goodness.

PILATE: On earth then the truth may not exist,
In your opinion?

JESUS: How can truth live on earth, tell me,
When so condemned on earth is he

By those who have authority
On earth, over reason?

PILATE: Lords, I find no cause, I fear,
To sentence this man that stands here.

CROWD: Crucify him! Crucify him!

PILATE: Shall I crucify your King?

CAIAPHAS: Pilate, do as we say you must:
Condemn to death this Jesus,
Or to Caesar we shall him entrust
And make your friendship cold.

CROWD: Crucify him!

(*Their cries rise to a tremendous climax.*)

PILATE: Now, that I am innocent of this blood shall ye see,
Both my hands completely washed shall be.

(*He signals for a bowl to be brought him and he washes his hands.*)

This blood will be dearly bought that ye spill so freely.

JEW: We pray that it may fall endlessly
On us and all our company.

CROWD: Yea, on us let it fall!

PILATE: Now your desires I shall fulfill,
Take him among you all,
On a cross put him in thrall
His ending there to make.

(JESUS *is led away.*)

THE CRUCIFIXION

CHARACTERS

JESUS
FOUR SOLDIERS

THE CRUCIFIXION

(JESUS *is given his cross and led through the crowd. He*
reaches Calvary and lays down his cross. Four SOLDIERS
enter with tools.)

1ST SOLDIER: Sir knights, take heed and hither hie
This task that now befall us four.
And know you now as well as I,
How the lords and leaders of our law
Have given doom this dope shall die.   *judgement*

2ND SOLDIER: Sir we've heard all that before!
But now we've come to Calvary,
Let's get on and say no more.

3RD SOLDIER: I am ready to do my lot,
And your commands I'll heed.

4TH SOLDIER: Just work out whose job is what,
And we shall do the deed.

1ST SOLDIER: Sirs, we had better start right soon,
If we are to any wages win.

2ND SOLDIER: He must be dead, needs must, by noon.

4TH SOLDIER: Then it is good time we begin.

3RD SOLDIER: Let's ding him down! Then he is done.   *knock*
He shall not daunt us with his din.

1ST SOLDIER: He needs a lesson, learn him one,
With care to him and all his kin.   *suffering*

2ND SOLDIER: The foulest death of all,
Shall this lad receive.

3RD SOLDIER: Yea, and on this cross so tall!

4TH SOLDIER: Come on then, roll up thy sleeve!

1ST SOLDIER: Yea, to this work we must take heed,
So that our working be not wrong.

2ND SOLDIER: Come on, dear friend, do take the lead,

181

We must to labour and get along.

3RD SOLDIER: And I have gone for gear, good speed,
Both hammers and nails, large and long.

4TH SOLDIER: Then may we boldly do this deed,
Come on, let's kill this traitor strong!

1ST SOLDIER: This lad is not the last
We shall nail upon the wood.

2ND SOLDIER: And we'll fasten him full fast,
For the general good.

3RD SOLDIER: Since every thing is right arrayed
Our work will wiser be.

4TH SOLDIER: This cross we have is well made
And even bored, for all to see.

1ST SOLDIER: Look that the lad on length be laid,
And then be tied unto this tree.

2ND SOLDIER: For all his boasts he shall be paid,
That you soon all shall see!

3RD SOLDIER: (*To* JESUS)

Come forth, thou cursed cur!
Thy comfort soon shall end!

4TH SOLDIER: Thy payment now thou wilt incur!

1ST SOLDIER: Walk on, I say! Attend!

JESUS: Almighty God, my Father free,
Let these matters be marked in mind;
Thou bade that I should ready be,
For Adam's plight I must be pined.   *tortured*
Here to death I do pledge me,
From that sin to save mankind,
And sovereignly beseech I thee
That they for me may favour find;
And from the fiend them fend,   *defend*
So that these souls be saved
In wealth without an end: *happiness*
I care naught else to crave.

182

1ST SOLDIER: Oh hark, sir knight, for Mahomet's blood!
    Of Adam's kin is all his thought.

2ND SOLDIER: The warlock waxes worse than wood.
    This doleful death he dreadeth nought.   *painful*

3RD SOLDIER: Thou shouldst have mind unto main and
        mood
    Of wicked works that thou hast wrought.

4TH SOLDIER: 'Tis pity thou didst not conclude
    To stop the lying tales thou taught.

1ST SOLDIER: Those lies he shall regret,
    And all his sauntering too.

2ND SOLDIER: Justice to him be met
    And death for all to view.

4TH SOLDIER: Come on, my boy, get off thy gown,
    And bend thy back unto this tree!

(JESUS *unfastens his gown and lies on the cross.*)

3RD SOLDIER: Behold, he himself has laid him down
    In length and breadth as he should be!

1ST SOLDIER: This traitor here be tainted of treason,
    Go fast and fetter him then, ye three;
    And, since he claims a kingdom's crown,
    Even as a king here, hang shall he!

2ND SOLDIER: For certain, I shall not cease
    Till his right hand be fast.

(*Taking his right hand*)

3RD SOLDIER: The left hand then's my piece,
    For I will not be last.

(*Taking his left hand*)

4TH SOLDIER: His limbs on length then shall I lead,
    And even unto the bore them bring.   *hole*

(*Going to his feet*)

1ST SOLDIER: Unto his head I shall take heed,

And with my hand help him to hang.

2ND SOLDIER: Now since we four shall do this deed,
And meddle with this unthrifty thing.
Let no man spare for special speed,
Till we have made an ending.

3RD SOLDIER: This forward may not fail,
Now we are right arrayed.   *properly prepared*

4TH SOLDIER: This boy here in our bail   *charge*
Shall bide full bitter braid.   *moments*

(*They tie* JESUS' *hands to the cross.*)

1ST SOLDIER: Sir knights, say now, work we ought?

2ND SOLDIER: Why sure, I hope. I hold this hand.

3RD SOLDIER: And to the bore I have it brought,
Full buxomly without band.

1ST SOLDIER: Strike on hard, for him thee bought.

2ND SOLDIER: Yes, here's a stub that will stiffly stand;   *nail*
Through bones and sinews it shall be sought.

(*A nail is hammered in* JESUS' *hand.*)

This work is well. Right grand!

1ST SOLDIER: Say sir, how do we use these?
This bargain we will win.

3RD SOLDIER: It fails a foot and more;
The sinews are so gone in.

4TH SOLDIER: I think the mark is wrongly bored.

2ND SOLDIER: Then must he bide in bitter bale.   *torment*

3RD SOLDIER: In faith it was too scantily scored
. That's why the hole doth fail.

1ST SOLDIER: Why carp ye so? Fast on a cord   *complain*
And tug him to, by top and tail.

(*They stretch the arm by means of a rope.*)

3RD SOLDIER: As thou commands us, haughty as a lord;

Come help us to haul him with ill hail!

1ST SOLDIER: Now for sure, that I shall do
Full quickly as a snail.

3RD SOLDIER: And I shall fasten him too,
Full nimbly with a nail.

(*Hammers nail into* JESUS' *hand.*)

This work will hold, that right neat.
His hands held fast I will contend.

4TH SOLDIER: Go then we all four to his feet,
'Tis well our time there we spend.

2ND SOLDIER: Let's see what jest his bale might beet.
Thereto my back now would I bend.

4TH SOLDIER: Oh! This work is all unmeet; *unfit*
This boring must we now amend.

1ST SOLDIER: Ah peace, man, for Mohamet,
Let no man know this wonder,
A rope shall pull him out
If all his sinews go asunder.

2ND SOLDIER: This cord here I have is strongly knit
For to do this job it surely will.

1ST SOLDIER: Hold it fast all ye that are fit.
And worry not, if his blood you spill.

2ND SOLDIER: Pull on ye both! Oh use your wit!

3RD SOLDIER: I shall not cease, I'll use my skill.

4TH SOLDIER: Dear sirs, let's hope he does not split!

2ND SOLDIER: Oh heave!

4TH SOLDIER: Ho now! Pull I still!

1ST SOLDIER: Have done, drive in that nail,
So that no fault be found.

4TH SOLDIER: This working would not fail
If four bulls here were bound.

1ST SOLDIER: These cords have much increased his pain,
They had to be so tight and taut.

2ND SOLDIER: Yea, see how stretched his flesh and veins,
On either side where we have fought.

3RD SOLDIER: Now all his tricks give him no gain
For all his sauntering he is here caught.

4TH SOLDIER: And I will go tell our sovereigns
Of all these works that we have wrought.

1ST SOLDIER: Nay, Sirs, another thing,
Falls first to you and me;
They bade we should him hang,
On high that men might see.

2ND SOLDIER: We know well what their words were
But, Sir, that deed will do us dear.

1ST SOLDIER: It will not help to argue more.
This rascal must hanged here.

2ND SOLDIER: The mortice is made fit therefore.

3RD SOLDIER: Fasten your fingers then, you hear.

4TH SOLDIER: Nay, we can never lift it there,
We will not raise it up this year.

1ST SOLDIER: Say, man, why carp'st thou so?
The lifting is but light.

2ND SOLDIER: I think there should be more
To heave him up on height.

3RD SOLDIER: Now sirs, I hope we will not need
More fellows here to help us try;
Methinks, we four should do the deed
And bear him up on high.

1ST SOLDIER: Now it must be done with all speed
No more chat, I will have no reply!
For this part shall I lift and lead,

186

On length he shall no longer lie.
Therefore now make no more sound,
Let us bear him to yon hill.

4TH SOLDIER: Then will I bear him down,
And tend his toes I will.

2ND SOLDIER: This cross will come out all cock-eyed,
And likely this lad will do it wrong.

3RD SOLDIER: I am ready, good sirs, abide.
I'll not fail, for I am strong.

1ST SOLDIER: Oh, stop your boasts and let me guide.
Lift up!

(*They lift the cross.*)

4TH SOLDIER: Let's see!

2ND SOLDIER: Oh, lift along!

3RD SOLDIER: From all this harm he would hide
If he were God.

4TH SOLDIER: The devil him hang!

1ST SOLDIER: Oh my Lord! Something cracked,
My shoulder must be torn.

2ND SOLDIER: And for sure I am whacked
So long I have this borne.

3RD SOLDIER: Oh, this load no longer will I twin.
For this cross doth weigh a ton.

4TH SOLDIER: Lay down again and leave your din;
This deed for us will ne'er be done.

(*They lay it down.*)

1ST SOLDIER: Sirs, let us see if some engine
Can be brought now we've begun.
For here should workers worship win
Our time for this is overrun!

2ND SOLDIER: Workers worthier than we
To find will be tough.

3RD SOLDIER: This labour right finishes me.
I'm proper out of puff.

4TH SOLDIER: Never have I come upon such a chore!
I think this cur has a spell cast.

2ND SOLDIER: My burden made me wondrous sore,
That to the hill I may not last.

1ST SOLDIER: Lift and he shall be there for sure.
Put your backs in it, fasten fast!

3RD SOLDIER: Oh, lift!

(*They lift the cross again.*)

1ST SOLDIER: We lo!

4TH SOLDIER: A little more!

2ND SOLDIER: Hold then!

1ST SOLDIER: How now!

2ND SOLDIER: The worst is past.

3RD SOLDIER: He weighs a wicked weight!

2ND SOLDIER: So may we all four say;
Here he was heard on height,
And raised in this array.

(*They have stood the cross up.*)

4TH SOLDIER: This made me bust my bollock stones
So boistrous was he for to bear.

1ST SOLDIER: Now let's raise him and no moans,
And set him by this mortice here,
And let him fall in as 'tis known
The pain for sure will have no peer.

3RD SOLDIER: Heave up!

4TH SOLDIER: Let down, for all his bones
Asunder now on all sides tear.

(JESUS *is now in place.*)

1ST SOLDIER: Say sir, how likes you now

This work that we have wrought?

4TH SOLDIER: We pray you say us how
Ye feel, or faint or aught?

JESUS: All men that walk by way or street,
Take care lest you forget this time.
Behold my head, my hands, my feet,
And fully feel now, were ye fine,
If any mourning may be meet
Or mischief measured unto mine.
My Father, that sits on holy seat,
Forgive these men that do unkind.
They know not what they do.
Therefore, my Father, I thee crave
Let these sins not them undo,
But see their souls to save.

1ST SOLDIER: Oh hark! He jangles like a jay!

2ND SOLDIER: Methinks he patters like a pie!   *magpie*

3RD SOLDIER: He has been doing so all day,
Mercy for others did he cry!

4TH SOLDIER: Is this the same that some did say
Was the Son of God on high?

1ST SOLDIER: Therefore he feels full fell away,
And deemed this day to die.   *was condemned*

3RD SOLDIER: Yea, let him hang there still
And make faces at the moon.

4TH SOLDIER: Then may we wend at will.

1ST SOLDIER: Nay – good sirs, not so soon.
Hold, there's another thing we need to do.
Which of you would this robe crave?

2ND SOLDIER: Nay sir, I rather we by lot drew
To see which of us it falls to have.

4TH SOLDIER: The short cut shall win what is due.
Whether it fall to knight or knave.

   (*They draw lots.*)

189

1ST SOLDIER: Brothers, look I have won!
  The mantle's mine, I say.

2ND SOLDIER: So our work here is done.
  Come let us wend our way.

(*Exeunt the* SOLDIERS, *leaving* JESUS *on the cross.*)

THE RESURRECTION
AND ASCENSION

2.

CHARACTERS

GOD

JESUS

MARY

PILATE

MARY MAGDALENE

THE RESURRECTION AND ASCENSION

(*Unseen by* JESUS, GOD *appears amongst the people and looks up at him.*)

JESUS: Now is my passion at an end.
        Father of Heaven, into thy hands
        I here my soul commend.

(GOD *departs.* JESUS *dies.* MARY *appears.*)

MARY: My dear son Jesus, raised on high,
        See how my heart is heavy as lead.
        I bid to thee a sweet good-bye,
        Alas, my darling son is dead.

        Alas, for my sweet son, I say,
        That dolefully to dead thus is dight.   *ready*
        Alas, for full lovely thou lay
        In my womb, thou worthy wight.   *man*
        Alas, that I should see this sight
        Of my son so still is he.
        Alas, that this blossom so bright
        Is falsely tied to this tree.
        Alas, my Lord, my life,
        With full great grief!
        They hang thee like a common thief.
        Alas!
        Thou that never did trespass!

PILATE: Woman! Do way of thy weeping.

(*To the audience*)

He that on yon hill hangs high
With guilt and shame, his blood to spill.
The blame for which is yours, not mine,
For 'crucify', was all your will.

And he that called himself a king,
With treason spoke he, all unshod.
But he died for another thing,
He called himself the Son of God.

(PILATE *laughs*.)

Now get ye from my sight!
And all the rest depart away,
There'll be no more to see this night.
Guards! Clear this place, I say!

(*To the sound of military drumming the audience and actors
are herded up and led by the soldiers to another place. The
disciples carry torches. Suddenly, far off, we hear the sound of
angels singing, and in a flood of light* JESUS *is revealed. He
approaches the crowd.* MARY MAGDALENE *seems unaware of*
JESUS, *she speaks as if to a stranger*.)

MARY MAGDALENE: Tell me gardener, I thee pray
If thou bore ought my Lord away.
Tell me the truth, say me not nay,
Where that he lies.
I shall remove him if I may
In any wise.

JESUS: Woman, why weepest thou? Be still.
Whom seekest thou? Tell me thy will,
Deny me not with nay.

MARY MAGDALENE: For my Lord I pine full ill.
The place his body now may fill
Tell me, I pray;
And I shall, if I may, his body bear with me
Unto my dying day, the better should I be.

JESUS: Why, what was he to thee in all truth now to say?

MARY MAGDALENE: Ah; dear he was to me that no longer
live I may.

JESUS: Mary, thou seekest thy God, and that am I.

MARY MAGDALENE: Raboni! My Lord so dear,
Now am I whole that thou art here.

(JESUS *turns to address the* DISCIPLES.)

JESUS: Peace be with you. It is I. Do not be afraid.
My brethren,

194

Go into the world, and by my grace
Preach my word in every place.
All those who steadfastly believe
Shall be saved, this I concede.
But whoso lives not by the law
And words that thou preach them before,
Damned shall be for evermore
With pains that they may never flee.

Now to my Father I am going.
You shall have here my blessing.

(JESUS *approaches the spot where we first saw* GOD, *with arms outstretched and with his back to the* DISCIPLES.)

All power in Heaven and Earth is given now to me.

(JESUS *turns to face the* DISCIPLES.)

Sweet my brethren, belov'd and dear,
To me is granted full power
O'er heaven and earth, both far and near,
For my godhead is most.
To teach all men now go ye,
And all the world will follow thee
In the name of my Father, and of me,
And of the Holy Ghost.

(GOD *appears above. Angels sing.* JESUS *ascends.*)

I ascend to my Father and to your Father,
My God and your God.
Lift up your hearts on high and cry!

ALL: Alleluia! Alleluia!

(GOD *greets* JESUS.)

GOD: My precious child, come unto me,
With me to live now shall ye wend,
There joy and bliss shall ever be,
Your life in liking, world without end.

Now is fulfilled all my forethought,
For ended is all earthly trace.
All worldly works that I have wrought

195

Are finished now, and in their place.
They that have sinned and ceased naught
Of sorrows great now shall they sing.
But they that mended while they might
Will live and dwell in my blessing.

I am Alpha and Omega,
The Life, the Way, the Truth,
The First and the Last.

FINIS.

Appendix

Of that tree's fruit ye may eat thy fill.
'Tis meet we journey with all haste
To yonder city without stop.

MARY: But, husband, I crave the fruit thereof.
Please fetch me some, from the tree top.

JOSEPH: I have no time to labour thus,
To pluck the fruit that here grows wild,
For this tree grows so high o'er us.
Let him give thee cherries that gave thee child.

MARY: Good Lord I pray, grant me this boon,
Give me these cherries if 'tis thy will.

(*The tree bends down.*)

I thank thee Lord, the tree bows low,
Now I mays't eat of it my fill.

JOSEPH: Lord, mercy, again I have offended thee,
Saying to my spouse unkind words thus.
For now I know, it may none other be
But that she bears the King of Bliss.

(*They travel on and enter Bethlehem; a man stands to greet them.*)

Worshipful sir, we bid thee good day.
Of Bethlehem ye seem to be.
Knowst thou a room wherein, I pray,
I may rest, and my wife Mary?

CITIZEN: Sir, this city is so full of late,
No room, know I, will thou find here.
But try against the city gate.

JOSEPH: I will; come on my, darling dear.
Ah, sweet my wife, what shall we do?
Where shall we lodge this night?

CITIZEN: Ho, sir, I have a stable, lo,
With beasts thou mayest spend the night.

MARY: Good husband, in haste, I say to you
My time is at an end,

Let's to the stable.

JOSEPH: Kind sir, adieu.

MARY: Husband, help me descend.

(*She dismounts from the donkey and together they enter the stable.*)

Now that I am in the stable brought,
I hope, right well, my child to see.
Go from me husband, I'll need thee naught.
Go from this place and leave me be.

(JOSEPH *goes out of the stable and tends the donkey.* MARY *goes to the back of the stable and kneels amongst the straw. After a moment, she returns to the front of the stable with the Baby Jesus in her arms. The stable fills with light. Angels sing.*)

MARY: Behold the child that God hath given,
Of God the incarnate Word.
Praise we now our King in heaven,
And thee, our infant Lord.

(*They all sing a carol.*)[1]

---

1. See Appendix.

The Passion

Bulgaria							
EU exp.	749	-21	81	949	1716	-16	101
EU imp.	922	9		845	1695	-8	
Balance	-173			104	21		
Romania							
EU exp.	2273	10	115	2056	4425	17	124
EU imp.	1981	18		1679	3574	5	
Balance	292			377	851		
Slovenia							
EU exp.	3048	14	134	2681	5339	3	126
EU imp.	2276	7		2130	4245	0	
Balance	772			551	1094		

1. Poland, Hungary, Czech Republic, Estonia, Slovenia

Bibliography

In recent years there has been a steady increase in the number of conferences, seminars, books and articles on enlargement of the EU and NATO. This section reviews some of the leading institutes working on enlargement, lists some of the more important works published and also includes a guide to the Commission and other web sites. It is not intended to be a comprehensive listing of all publications on enlargement.

Amongst the research community in Europe, the Centre for European Policy Studies (CEPS) in Brussels, the Centre for Economic Policy Research (CEPR) in London, the Bertelsmann Foundation in Gütersloh, the Royal Institute of International Affairs (Chatham House) in London, the Netherlands Institute for International Relations (Clingendael), the WEU Institute for Security Studies (Paris), the Sussex European Institute, the Centre for European Reform (CER) in London, and the European University Institute in Florence have been prominent in publishing works on enlargement.

One of the most comprehensive works is a series of essays edited by Marc Maresceau (1997) and based on a colloquium at Ghent in 1996. The essays analyse the Europe Agreements and the preaccession strategy and also cover the IGC. Peter Ludlow (1997) of CEPS has written a critical account of the Commission's approach in his book. Alan Mayhew (1997), a former Director in the Commission, provides a cost–benefit analysis of enlargement. The Bertelsmann Foundation have published an annual review of the candidate countries' preparations for enlargement. Werner Weidenfeld (1997) edited the latest edition. The Foundation has also published 'A new Ostpolitik—Strategies for a United Europe', challenging European leaders to consider the historic dimensions of enlargement. Richard Baldwin has written extensively on the problems surrounding enlargement, including his 1994 *Towards an Integrated Europe*. John Eatwell (1997) and fellow authors Michael Ellman, Mats Karlsson, Mario Nuti and Judith Shapiro also argue for a wider view of costs and benefits. The security aspects of enlargement have been covered by Monika Wohlfeld (1997). William Wallace covers EU and NATO enlargement in his CER essay 'Opening the Door (1997)' whilst the Bertelsmann Foundation report on 'CFSP and Enlargement' (1995) assesses the implications of enlargement for the EU's nascent foreign and security policy.

Both the authors of this book have published numerous articles on enlargement including Cameron's 'The Fourth Enlargement' (1994), 'Enlargement—a Challenge for Europe', *ELIAMEP Occasional Paper*, Autumn, 1996, and with G. Burghardt 'The Enlargement of the European Union' in *European External Affairs Review*, Spring 1997. Avery (1994) covers the procedural aspects of enlargement negotiations. Kirsty Hughes (1996) has provided another good overview in 'Preparing for Enlargement' (1997). From the candidates' perspective Andras Inotai has been a prolific exponent of their position.

The European Commission has also improved its web site in the Europa Server and many documents, including Agenda 2000, are available at *http://europa.eu.int*. There were more than 120,000 visits to the Agenda 2000 site between 16 July and the end of August 1997. NATO has a good web site at *http://www.nato.int*, and the WEU also has a web site at *http:// www.fco.gov.uk/weu/purpose.html*.

BOOKS

Baldwin, Richard,*Towards an Integrated Europe* (London: CEPR, 19940.

Baldwin, Richard, P. Haaparanta and J. Klander, *Expanding Membership of the European Community* (Cambridge: Cambridge University Press, 1995).

Bulmer, Simon, and Andrew Scott (eds.), *Economic and Political Integration in Europe* (Oxford: Blackwell, 1994).

Eatwell, John *et al.* (eds.), *Not 'Just Another Accession'—'The Political Economy of Enlargement to the East'* (London: IPPR, 1997).

Ludlow, Peter, *Preparing Europe for the 21st Century* (Brussels: CEPS, 1997).

Maresceau, Marc (ed.), *Enlarging the European Union* (London: Longman, 1997).

Mayhew Alan, *Recreating Europe; Relations between the European Union and the Countries of Central and Eastern Europe* (Cambridge: Cambridge University Press, 1997).

Preston, Christopher, *Enlargement and Integration in the European Union* (London: Routledge, 1977).

Weidenfeld, Werner (ed.), *Central and Eastern Europe on the way into the European Union* (Gütersloh: Bertelsmann Foundation, 1997).

ARTICLES, CHAPTERS AND MONOGRAPHS

Adameic, J., *East-Central Europe and the European Community: A Polish Perspective* (RIIA Discussion Paper no. 47; London: Royal Institute of International Affairs, 1993).

Agence Europe, 27 October 1997; 5 December 1997; 9 December 1997; 14 December 1997.

Altmann F-L., W. Andreff and G. Fink, *Future Expansion of the European Union in Central Europe* (IEF [Research Institute for European Affairs] Working Paper no. 8; Vienna: University of Economics and Business Administration, 1996).

Anderson, K., and R. Tyres, *Implication of EC Expansion for European Agricultural Policies, Trade and Welfare* (CEPR Discussion Paper no. 829; London: Centre for Economic Policy Research, 1993).

Asmus, Ronald D., Richard L. Kugler, and Stephen Larrabee, 'NATO Expansion: The Next Steps', *Survival*, 37.1 (1995), pp. 7-33.

Avery, Graham,'The European Union's Enlargement Negotiations', *The Oxford International Review*, 5.3 (1994), pp. 27-32.

—'The Commission's Perspective on the (EFTA Accession) Negotiations' (SEI Working paper no. 12; Brighton: Sussex European Institute, University of Sussex, 1995).

Balázs, P., *The EU's Collective Regional Approach to its Eastern Enlargement: Consequences and Risks* (CORE Working Paper no. 1/1997; Copenhagen: Copenhagen Research Project on European Integration, 1997).

Baldwin, Richard, 'The Growth Effects of 1992', *Economic Policy* 2 (1989), pp. 247-81.

Baldwin, Richard, Joseph Francois and Richard Portes, 'The Costs and Benefits of Eastern Enlargement', *Economic Policy Journal*, April 1997.

Barrett, John, 'NATO Reform: Alliance Policy and Cooperative Security', in Ingo Peters (ed.), *New Security Challenges: The Adaptation of International Institutions* (Münster: Verlag, 1996), pp. 123-51.

Bárta, Vit, and Sándor Richter, *Eastern Enlargement of the EU from a Western and an Eastern Perspective* (Vienna: WIIW, 1996)

Bertelsmann Foundation, *CFSP and Enlargement* (Bertelsmann Foundation: Gütersloh, 1995)

Besnainou Denis, (1995) 'Les Fonds Structurels: Quelle application aux PECO?' *Economie Internationale—Centre d'Etudes Prospectives et d'Informations Internationales* (Paris: Centre d'Etudes, 1995).

Bofinger, P., *The Political Economy of the Eastern Enlargement of the EU* (CEPR Discussion Paper no. 1234; London: Centre for Economic Policy Research, 1995).

Borawski, John, 'If not NATO Enlargement: What does Russia Want?' *European Security* 5.3 (1996), pp. 381-95.

Brabant, Jozef M van., *Bonding the EU and the Transition Economies* (London: United Nations 1996).

Brenton, P., and D. Gros, *The Budgetary Implications of EC Enlargement* (CEPS Working Document no. 78; Centre for European Policy Studies; Brussels, 1993).

Broek, Hans van den, 'Enlargement of the EU', *Financial Times*, 22 September 1997.

Buckwell, *et al.*, *Feasibility of an Agricultural Strategy to Prepare the Countries of Central and East European Europe for EU Accession* (Study prepared for DG-1 of the Commission; Wye, Kent, 1994).

Burghardt, G., and F. Cameron, 'The Enlargement of the European Union', *European External Affairs Review* 2 (1997), pp. 7-23.

Cadot, O., and J. de Melo, 'France and the CEECs: Adjusting to Another Enlargement', in R. Faini and R. Portes (eds.), *European Union Trade with Eastern Europe: Adjustment and Opportunities* (Centre for Economic Policy Research: London, 1995).

Cameron, Fraser, 'The Fourth Enlargement in the European Union', *Journal of Common Market Studies* 33 (1994), pp. 17-34.

Centre for Finnish Business and Policy Studies, *More Members for the EU?* (Helsinki: CFBPS, 1997).

CEPR, *Is Bigger Better? The Economics of EC Enlargement* (Monitoring European Integration, 3; London: Centre for Economic Policy Research, 1992).

Chavigny, Régis, 'Les perspectives d'intégration des pays d'Europe centrale et orientale dans l'Union Européenne', *Revue d'études comparatives Est-Ouest* 4 (1996), pp. 36-52.

Dannreuther, Roland, *Eastward Enlargement—NATO and the EU* (Oslo: Institut for Forsvarsstudier, 1997).

Dauderstädt, Michael, and Barbara Lippert, *Europe 2000: No Integration without Differentiation* (London; Friedrich Ebert Stiftung Institute, 1996).

Daviddi, R., and F. Ilzkovitz, *The Eastern Challenge of Enlargement of the European Union: Major Challenges for Macroeconomic Policies and Institutions of Central and East European Countries* (Paper presented at the Eleventh Annual Congress of the European Economic Association, 21–24 August 1996).

Delpeuch, Jean-Luc, 'Intégration européenne et développement économique', *Revue d'études comparatives Est-Ouest* 4 (1996), pp. 53-69.

Deszéri, Kálmán, *The Visegrad-4 and the European Union: Accession and Financial Transfers* (Budapest: Institute of World Economics, 1996).

Division of Foreign Policy Research, *The Costs of Eastern Enlargement of the EU are Exaggerated* (Bonn: Friedrich Ebert Foundation, 1996).

Drábek, Z., and A. Smith, *Trade Performance and Trade Policy in Central and Eastern Europe* (CEPR Discussion Paper no. 1182; London: Centre for Economic Policy Research, 1995).

Ehlermann, C-D., *Increased Differentiation or Stronger Uniformity* (Robert Schuman Centre Working Paper no. 95/21; Florence: European University Institute, 1995).

Faini, R., and Richard Portes (eds.) *European Union Trade with Eastern Europe: Adjustment and Opportunities* (London: Centre for Economic Policy Research, 1995).

Faini, R., and A. Venturini, *Migration and Growth: The Experience of Southern Europe* (CEPR Discussion Paper no. 964; London: Centre for Economic Policy Research, 1994).

Feldman, Gardner Lily, *The Political and Economic Integration of Central and Eastern Europe: The European Union's Enlargement Project and EU–US Co-operation* (Washington, DC: Georgetown University, 1996).

Fingleton, John, Eleanor Fox, Damien Neven and Paul Seabright, *Report on Competition Policy in Central and Eastern European Countries* (London: Centre for Economic Policy Research, 1995).

Hagen, Jürgen von, *The Political Economy of Eastern Enlargement of the EU* (London: CEPR, October 1996).

Halpern, L., *Comparative Advantage and Likely Trade Patterns of the CEECs* (CEPR Discussion Paper no. 1003; London: Centre for Economic Policy Research, 1994).

Halpern, L., and C. Wyplosz, *The Role of Exchange Rates in the Process of Economic Transformation* (CEPR Discussion Paper no. 1145; London: Centre for Economic Policy Research, 1995).

Hamilton, C.B., and L.A. Winters, 'Opening up International Trade with Eastern Europe', *Economic Policy*, 14 (1992), pp. 14-27.

Hare, Paul, *How Far is Eastern Europe from Brussels? Reform deficits in Potential Member States* (Edinburgh: Heriot-Watt University, 1996).

Holmes P., A. Smith and A.R. Young, *Regulatory Convergence between the European Union and Central and Eastern Europe* (Unpublished manuscript; University of Sussex, Brighton, 1996).

House of Lords, *The Implications for Agriculture of the Europe Agreements*, Session 1993–94 10th Report, Select Committee on the European Communities (London: HMSO, 1994).

Hughes, Kirsty, *Eastward Enlargement of the EU: EU Strategy and Future Challenges* (RIIA European Programme Working Paper no. 2; London: Royal Institute for International Affairs, 1996).

Hughes, Kirsty, and Heather Grabbe, *The Impact of Enlargement on EU Trade and Industrial Policy* (London: Royal Institute of International Affairs, 1996).

Inotai, András, *From Association Agreements to Full Membership? The Dynamics of Relations between the Central and East European Countries and the European Union* (Budapest: Hungarian Academy of Sciences, 1995).

Italianer, A., 'Whither the Gains from European Economic Integration?', *Revue économique*, 45.3 (1994), pp. 36-49.

Jackson, M., and J. Swinnen, *A Statistical Analysis of the Current Situation of Agriculture in Central and East European Countries* (Report to EU Commission, DG-1; Leuven: Katholeike Universiteit, 1994).

Jopp, Mathias, *The Strategic Implications of European Integration* (Adelphi Paper no. 290; London: Brassey's, 1994).

Josling, Tim, and Peter Walkenhorst, *Can the CAP Survive Enlargement to the East?* (Stanford, CA: Stanford University Press, 1995).

Kawecka-Wyrzykowska, Elzbieta, *On the Benefits of the Accession for Western and Eastern Europe* (Warsaw: Foreign Trade Institute, 1996).

Kumar, Andrej, (1996) *The CEE Countries' Aspirations for Enlargement* (University of Ljubljana, 1996).

Laurent, Alain, (1996) *L'elargissement de l'Union Européenne aux PECO: bilans et perspectives* (Report prepared for DATAR, October 1996).

Le Cacheux, Jacques (ed.), *L'Union Européenne: les Conséquences Économiques et Budgétaires de l'Elargissement à l'Est* (Paris: Observatoire Français des Cononctures Economiques, n.d.).

—*Europe, La Nouvelle Vague: Perspectives économiques de l'elargissement* (Paris: Presses de Sciences Politiques, 1996).

Mahé, L., H. Cordier, H. Guyomard and T. Roe, 'L'agriculture et l'élargissement de la Union européenne aux pays d'Europe centrale et orientale: transition en vue de l'intégration ou intégration pour la transition' (Study prepared for DG-1 of the Commission; Rennes: INRA, 1994).

Mato, Zsolt-Istvan, 'The Case against NATO Enlargement', *Transition* 21 (1997), pp. 28-31.

Mihalka, Michael, 'Continued Resistance to NATO Expansion', *Transition* 14 (1995), pp. 36-41.

Neven, D., *Trade Liberalisation with Eastern Nations: How Sensitive?* (CEPR Discussion Paper no. 1000; London: Centre for Economic Policy Research, 1994).

Nuti, D.M., 'Hidden and Repressed Inflation in Soviet-type Economies: Definitions, Measurement and Stabilisation', *Contributions to Political Economy* 5 (1986), pp. 37-82.

Petrakos, G.C., 'The Regional Dimension in Central and East European Countries: An Assessment', *East European Economies* (September–October 1996), pp. 66-85.

Pridham, Geoffrey, 'The International Dimension of Democratisation: Theory, Practice and Inter-Regional Comparisons', in Geoffrey Pridham, Eric Herring and G. Sanford (eds.), *Building Democracy? The International Dimension of Democratisation in Eastern Europe* (London: Leicester University Press, 1994).

Rollo, J., and A. Smith, 'The Political Economy of EC Trade with Eastern Europe: Why So Sensitive?', *Economic Policy* (April 1993), pp. 140-81.

Samson, Ivan, 'Pôles de croissance et de décision à l'Est: 1994–2015' (Study prepared for *DATAR*, October 1996).

Schumacher, D., and U. Moebius, 'Analysis of Community Trade Barriers Facing Central and Eastern Europe and Impact of the Europe Agreements', in EC Commission, *The Economic Interpenetration between the European Community and Eastern Europe* (Luxembourg: European Economy Reports and Studies, no. 6, 1994).

Sedelmeier, Ulrich, 'The European Union's Association Policy towards Central and Eastern Europe: Political and Economic rationales', in *Conflict* (SEI Working Paper no. 7: 1994).

Senior Nello, S.M., 'The European Union and Central-East Europe: Background to the Enlargement Question', in *idem*, *L'Unione européenne face au defi de l'élargissment* (Luxembourg: Institut Universitaire International, 1997).

Smith, A., P. Holmes, U. Sedelmeier, E. Smith, H. Wallace and R. Young, *The European Union and Central and Eastern Europe: Pre-Accession Strategies* (SEI Working Paper no. 15; Brighton: Sussex European Institute, 1996).

Smith, K., 'The Making of Foreign Policy in the European Community/Union: The Case of Eastern Europe 1988–95' (PhD dissertation; London: LSE, 1996).

Steinherr, Alfred, 'The Pivotal Role of the European Union for Central and Eastern Europe', *Swiss Journal of Economics and Statistics* (1995), pp. 303-27.

Tangermann, S., and Tim Josling, *Pre-accession Agricultural Policies for Central Europe and the European Union* (Study prepared for DG-1 of the Commission; Göttingen and Stanford, 1994).

Tarditi S., J. Marsh and S.M. Senior Nello, *Agricultural Strategies for the Enlargement of the European Union to Central and Eastern Europe* (Study prepared for DG-1 of the Commission; Siena, 1994).

Tracy, M. (ed.), *East–West Agricultural Trade: The Impact of the Association Agreements.* (La Hutte, Belgium: APS, 1994).

Trenin Dmitri, 'Avoiding a new confrontation with NATO', *NATO Review* (May 1996), pp. 17-20.

Tyres, R., *Economic Reform in Europe and the Soviet Union: Implications for International Food Markets* (Washington, DC: IFPRI, 1993).

Van den Bempt, P. and G. Theelen (eds.), *From Europe Agreements to Accession.* (Brussels: European Interuniversity Press, 1996).

Wallace, Helen, and William Wallace, *Flying Together in a Larger and More Diverse European Union* (Working Document 87; The Hague: Netherlands Scientific Council for Government Policy, 1995).

Wallace, Helen, 'Fitting the European Union for Europe' in Frank Vibert (ed.), *Perspectives on Europe* (London: European Policy Forum, 1996)

Wallace, William, *Opening the Door* (Centre for European Reform: London, 1997).

Wang, Z.H., and L. Alan Winters, *The Trading Potential of Eastern Europe* (CEPR Discussion Paper no. 610; London: Centre for Economic Policy Research, 1995).

Weise, Christian, 'Reforms Necessary if Eastern Enlargement of the EU is to be Financed', *DIW Economic Bulletin*, 34.1 (1997). Study commissioned by the German Federal Ministry of Economics.

Winters, L. Alan, 'The Europe Agreements: With a Little Help from Our Friends', in *The Association Process: Making it Work* (Centre for Economic Policy Research Occasional Paper no. 11; London, 1992) , pp. 17-33.

Wohlfeld, Monika, *The Effects of Enlargement on Bilateral Relations in Central and Eastern Europe* (Chaillot Papers, 26; Paris: Institute for Security Studies, 1997).

Yavlinski, Grigorii , 'The NATO Distraction', *Transition*, 21 March (1997), pp. 32-34.

Zagorski, Andrei, 'NATO and CIS: A Russian View' *Cambridge Review of International Affairs* 8.2 (1995), pp. 101-23.

EU AND COMMISSION DOCUMENTS

CdR (1997) Opinion on the Effects of Enlargement on the Union's Policies, CdR 280/97, Committee of the Region, Brussels.

EC Commission (1994) *The Europe Agreements and Beyond: A Strategy to Prepare the countries of Central and Eastern Europe for Accession,* COM(94) 320 final.

EC Commission (1995) *Study on Alternatives for the Development of Relations in the Field of Agriculture between the EU and the Associated Countries with a View to*

Future Accession of these Countries. Agricultural Strategy Paper, CSE (95) 607, Brussels.

EC Commission (1995) *Preparation of the Associated Countries of Central and Eastern Europe for Integration into the Internal Market of the Union,* COM (95) 163 final, 3 May.

EC Commission (1995) *Interim Report from the Commission to the European Council on the Effects on the Policies of the European Union of Enlargement to the Associated Countries of Central and Eastern Europe,* CSE(95) 605.

EC Commission (1996) *Reinforcing Political Union and Preparing for Enlargement,* COM (96) 90 final, 28 February.

EC Commission (1996) 'The Improvement in the External Situation of the Central–East European countries. Supplement A' *Economic Analyses,* 7, July.

EC Commission (1997) 'Agenda 2000—For a Stronger and Wider Union', *Bulletin of the European Union,* supplement 5/97.

EC Commission (1997) 'Commission Opinion on Hungary's Application for Membership of the European Union', *Bulletin of the European Union,* supplement 6/97.

EC Commission (1997) 'Commission Opinion on Poland's Application for Membership of the European Union', *Bulletin of the European Union,* supplement 7/97.

EC Commission (1997) Commission Opinion on Romania's Application for Membership of the European Union', *Bulletin of the European Union,* supplement 8/97.

EC Commission (1997) Commission Opinion on Slovakia's Application for Membership of the European Union, *Bulletin of the European Union,* supplement 9/97.

EC Commission (1997) 'Commission Opinion on Latvia's Application for Membership of the European Union, *Bulletin of the European Union,* supplement 10/97.

EC Commission (1997) 'Commission Opinion on Estonia's Application for Membership of the European Union', *Bulletin of the European Union,* supplement 11/97.

EC Commission (1997) 'Commission Opinion on Lithuania's Application for Membership of the European Union', *Bulletin of the European Union,* supplement 12/97.

EC Commission (1997) 'Commission Opinion on Bulgaria's Application for Membership of the European Union', *Bulletin of the European Union,* supplement 13/97.

EC Commission (1997) 'Commission Opinion on Czech Republic's Application for Membership of the European Union', *Bulletin of the European Union,* supplement 14/97.

EC Commission (1997) 'Commission Opinion on Slovenia's Application for Membership of the European Union', *Bulletin of the European Union,* supplement 15/97.

European Commission, (1995) *Interim report from the Commission to the European Council on the Effects on the Policies of the European Union of Enlargement to the Associated Countries of Central and Eastern Europe,* CSE (95) 605, Brussels 6.12.1995.

European Commission, (1995) *Study on Alternative Strategies for the Development of Relations in the field of Agriculture between the EU and the Associated Countries of Central and Eastern Europe with a View to Future Accession of these Countries,* CSE (95) 607, Brussels, 6.12.1995.

EcoSoc (1997) Opinion on the Enlargement of the European Union, Economic and Social Committee, Brussels.

Journal of Common Market Studies

Incorporating The European Union: Annual Review

Published by Blackwell Publishers in association with the University Association for Contemporary European Studies

Edited by Iain Begg and John Peterson

The *Journal of Common Market Studies* is a leading journal in the field, publishing high quality, accessible articles on the latest EU issues. For more than 30 years *JCMS* has been _the_ forum for the development and evaluation of theoretical and empirical issues in the politics and economics of integration, focussing principally on developments within the European Union. *JCMS* aims to achieve a disciplinary balance between political science and economics, including the various sub-disciplines such as monetary economics, fiscal policy, political economy, public policy studies, public administration and international relations. In addition to mainstream theoretical and empirical articles, *JCMS* publishes shorter pieces which focus on specific policy areas or which report the results of specialised research projects.

Journal of Common Market Studies ISSN: 0021-9886. Volume 38 (2000) contains 5 issues plus a free subscription to the Annual Review.

A library subscription to the print volume entitles readers to:

Free access to full text articles online

Free copying for non-commercial course packs

Free access to all available electronic back volumes

Special terms are available for libraries in purchasing consortia.

Contact e-help@blackwellpublishers.co.uk

BLACKWELL
Publishers

108 Cowley Road, Oxford OX4 1JF, UK
350 Main Street, Malden, MA 02148, USA
jnlinfo@blackwellpublishers.co.uk

Visit our website for contents listings, abstracts, samples, and to subscribe

www.blackwellpub.com

UNIVERSITY ASSOCIATION FOR CONTEMPORARY EUROPEAN STUDIES
UACES Secretariat, King's College London, Strand, London WC2R 2LS
Tel: 0171 240 0206 Fax: 0171 836 2350 E-mail: uaces@compuserve.com
http://www.uaces.org/u-info/

UACES

University Association for Contemporary European Studies

THE ASSOCIATION

- Brings together academics involved in researching Europe with representatives of government, industry and the media who are active in European affairs
- Primary organisation for British academics researching the European Union
- Over 500 individual and corporate members from Dept such as Politics, Law, Economics & European Studies, plus a growing number of Graduate Students who join as Associate Members

MEMBERSHIP BENEFITS

- Individual Members eligible for special highly reduced fee for The Journal of Common Market Studies
- Regular Newsletter - events and developments of relevance to members
- Conferences - variety of themes, modestly priced, further reductions for members
- Publications, including the new series *Contemporary European Studies*, from May 1998
- Research Network, and research conference
- Through the European Community Studies Association (ECSA), access to a larger world wide network
- Information Documentation & Resources eg: The Register of Courses in European Studies and the Register of Research into European Integration

Current Cost of Membership per annum - Individual Members - £20.00; Graduate Students £10.00;
Corporate Members £40.00 (2 copies of documentation sent and any 2 members of Dept / Organisation eligible to attend conferences at Members' rate)

APPLICATION FOR MEMBERSHIP OF UACES

Please indicate if you wish to receive details of the JCMS ☐

I enclose Banker's Order / cheque for £ _____ payable to UACES

Name _____

Faculty / Dept _____

Institution _____

Address _____

_____

Tel No: _____

Fax No: _____

E-mail: _____

Signature & Date _____

Address for correspondence if different:

_____

_____

BANKER'S ORDER FORM

Please return to UACES and not to your Bank

TO_____(Bank)

_____(Sort Code)

AT _____(Address)

_____

Please pay to Lloyds Bank (30-00-08), Pall Mall Branch, 3-10 Waterloo Place London SW1Y 4BE

in favour of UACES Account No 3781242

on the _____day of _____

the sum of £20 (TWENTY POUNDS) and the same sum on the same date each year until countermanded

Signature & Date _____ _____

Account No _____

Name _____

Address _____

_____